Handwritten inscription:

Jan. 10 – 2010

Dear TRISH –

How wonderful being in this creative experience with you – ARTIST IN Residence!

I hope you will have much fun exploring this book!

With love –
Linda ♥

The PAINTING PATH

Embodying Spiritual Discovery through Yoga, Brush and Color

Linda Novick

Foreword by Richard Segalman

Walking Together, Finding the Way®
SKYLIGHT PATHS®
PUBLISHING
Woodstock, Vermont

The Painting Path:
Embodying Spiritual Discovery through Yoga, Brush and Color

2007 First Printing
© 2007 by Linda Novick

For information regarding permission to reprint material from this book, please mail or fax your request in writing to SkyLight Paths Publishing, Permissions Department, at the address / fax number listed below, or e-mail your request to permissions@skylightpaths.com.

Grateful acknowledgment is given for permission to use material from the following sources: "Breath by Breath" by Danna Faulds. © 2003 by Danna Faulds. Reprinted by permission. *Sunburst* by Anne Katzeff. Reprinted by permission. *Japan Memories* and *Self-Portrait* by Laura Riegelhaupt. Reprinted by permission.

Library of Congress Cataloging-in-Publication Data

Novick, Linda.
The painting path : embodying spiritual discovery through yoga, brush, and color / Linda Novick.
     p. cm.
ISBN-13: 978-1-59473-226-3 (quality pbk.)
ISBN-10: 1-59473-226-4 (quality pbk.)
1. Art—Technique. 2. Art—Psychological aspects. 3. Spirituality. 4. Yoga. I. Title.

N7430.5.N68 2007
751.4—dc22

2007029268

10 9 8 7 6 5 4 3 2 1

Manufactured in Canada
Cover Design: Melanie Robinson
Cover Art: *Berkshire View with Daisies and Purple Mountain* by Linda Novick

SkyLight Paths Publishing is creating a place where people of different spiritual traditions come together for challenge and inspiration, a place where we can help each other understand the mystery that lies at the heart of our existence.

SkyLight Paths sees both believers and seekers as a community that increasingly transcends traditional boundaries of religion and denomination—people wanting to learn from each other, *walking together, finding the way.*

SkyLight Paths, "Walking Together, Finding the Way" and colophon are trademarks of LongHill Partners, Inc., registered in the U.S. Patent and Trademark Office.

Walking Together, Finding the Way®
Published by SkyLight Paths Publishing
A Division of LongHill Partners, Inc.
Sunset Farm Offices, Route 4, P.O. Box 237
Woodstock, VT 05091
Tel: (802) 457-4000   Fax: (802) 457-4004
www.skylightpaths.com

Contents

Foreword   v

Introduction   1

1 REMEMBERING YOUR ARTIST SELF
Playful Experimentation with Oil Pastels   13

2 WHAT'S REAL?
Looking beneath the Surface with Drawing   25

3 GETTING IN TOUCH
Discovering What We Really Want with Watercolors   46

4 YOUR CIRCLE OF POWER
Rediscovering Your Authentic Vision with Resist   63

5 STEPPING BACK
Cultivating Witness Consciousness Using Soft Pastels   76

6 STAYING FLEXIBLE
Practicing Improvisation with Liquefying Pastels   96

7 PURPOSEFUL DIRECTION
Practicing Beginner's Mind with Batik   110

8 UNCOVERING YOUR DREAMS
Discovering the Power of Images through Collage   132

9 BUT DOES IT LOOK LIKE ME?
Practicing Nonjudgment with Self-Portrait   146

10 LISTENING TO OUR INTUITION
Nurturing Courage through Oil Paints   162

11 THE STORIES WE TELL
Reinterpreting Our Lives through
Painted Autobiography   180

Conclusion: The Painting Path Continues   194
Resources   196

Foreword

I relocated to the Hudson Valley about thirty-five years ago. I was not too familiar with the large heroic landscapes of F. E. Church and the Hudson Valley School of Art. Their vision was almost too overwhelming. I then began to see and feel the beauty they captured. Still, there was something missing. I traveled around and began to see the small, intimate cities and towns of the Valley. Why wasn't someone working with these interesting buildings? There was always Charles Burchfield's American Scene paintings to turn to, but I wanted a more intimate voice. I am not usually a landscape painter, but I began to see possibilities.

I then saw a watercolor by Linda Novick and everything changed. Whenever there was an exhibition that included her work, I went to see it. I began to see Upstate New York through her eyes. I saw bridges and alleys, factories and old buildings come alive. It is hard to see things with a fresh vision when other influences are so strong. I did try to work on some of the images that presented themselves to me, but Linda had claim to them.

I then met her at sketch classes. I realized she was not only a painter, but she liked to draw too. I felt an instant respect and admiration. She was an admirer of my masters, Edgar Degas, John Singer Sargent, Joaquin Sorolla and many contemporary painters. We became fast friends, and I watched her vision grow and change over the years. I admired her discipline and dedication.

Many of her paintings are still in my head: empty streets that painter Edward Hopper would identify with, wonderful paintings of pool players at their game, a small Mexican painting I own and look at every day. Linda Novick's vision is so strong that I see certain streets and buildings through her eyes.

When I started to do yoga many years ago, I was immediately taken with the body, mind, and spiritual connection it provided, which is so similar to the connection we can feel through making art. It is no accident that Linda feels this too; to let go and let the muses in, is a worthy achievement. Linda is doing this with her painting and teaching. She is still growing as a person and painter.

Whenever I see Linda Novick, I smile. She is one of the lucky ones who has managed to make her art her life.

Richard Segalman
Woodstock, New York

Introduction

In the forty-five years that I have been an artist and art teacher, I have found that people who express themselves by painting are pretty happy people. I know from my personal experience that when I am working on a painting I can hardly wait for the next day so I can return to it. If I'm working on a batik, I can't wait to see how the last color I dyed has dried. If I'm working on a pastel or oil painting, the first thing I do upon waking is run to my easel to see how it looks. Sometimes it looks much better than the day before, and sometimes an area needs improvement.

But whatever the state of my work that day, working on a painting makes me return to the excitement I felt as a young child when everything was an adventure and the world was a fresh and exciting place. When we are painting, there is so much to look forward to. While we have a work in progress, we have a passion, a goal   something that makes our heart sing!

I'm not alone in this feeling. Often my art students, many of whom began painting as adults, have told me that taking up painting revolutionized their lives by helping them tap into inner resources and an inner creativity they never knew they had. But it's more than that. Many of them discover a depth of joy when painting that they never had before. Painting is a powerful tool that can help us to access our spirit.

In this book, you will be introduced to painting projects that will help you discover your spirituality and build a direct link to your creativity. We will inquire into the meaning of spirit and investigate our connection to it. In each chapter you will sample a different art project, beginning with a playful exploration of oil pastels and culminating in an autobiographical painting project that you will design and execute yourself using the techniques you will learn throughout the book.

The projects I have chosen are somewhat eclectic and are designed to progress from relatively simple to more challenging. But don't worry. This book is for everyone regardless of your level of experience with painting. If you are a complete novice, you can take the projects slowly as you enhance your skills. If you are already a painter, these projects will sharpen your skills, give you new ideas, and generally help you celebrate the act of painting even as you discover new ways it can nurture your spirit and transform your life.

WHY YOGA?

In addition to the art projects, each chapter includes a body-centered experience that is designed to help you flow more easily into each art exercise. These simple stretching and breathing exercises are inspired by the ancient practice of yoga, which incorporates breathing and movement to unify mind, body, and spirit. Through the practices of conscious breathing, gentle stretching, and massage, you will recharge your body and focus your mind and thereby experience renewed energy and clarity as you explore the art projects.

I have chosen these particular exercises for two reasons. First, you will find them accessible and easy to do whether or not you have had any experience with yoga movements. All our body-centered practices are designed to help you relax, develop concentration, and create open channels to creativity and greater self-expression. Second, each fits with the spiritual theme of the chapter and will help you prepare for the art project that follows it.

For example, in chapter 9, you will focus on looking at yourself without judgment. For the body-centered experience, you will massage your face with an attitude of curiosity and objectivity. By tenderly using your fingers to massage your face, you not only treat yourself gently, you also prepare yourself for the painting experience, which is to paint your portrait using a mirror. Having prepared yourself in this way, you can both release judgments you may have about your appearance and get to know yourself on a level deeper than the superficial view you get when you gaze into a mirror. This exercise will give you an entirely different perspective of your face, which can be expressed in the self-portrait you paint.

In some cases, I have also provided alternative methods for doing the exercises so that you can do them even if you have limited mobility. Feel free to pick and choose the exercises that call to you.

WHY PAINTING?

Spiritual discovery is a very personal journey for everyone and comes in different forms. Some people find themselves connecting to their spirituality when they are in a church, synagogue, mosque, or other places of worship, while others have transcendent experiences when they are in nature or in the presence of animals or children. Still others find a connection to their spirituality in sports, dancing, martial arts, or yoga. In this book you will discover how you can access your spirituality.

When we are young, we have a sense of the world that is vivid and transcendent, but many of us forget how to access that experience. Responsibilities and the fast pace of daily life often whisk us away from contemplative times alone and from activities that bring us peace and joy. Yoga slows our bodies down, and when our bodies relax, our minds are able to relax.

In this respect, painting has much in common with yoga. Painting is a very physical form of art, one filled with tactile sensations. If you're like me, there's nothing that you like better than squeezing out a brand new tube of cadmium red oil paint. As I watch the line of paint coil up, so vibrant and juicy, I just want to *touch* it. Painting, like yoga, has a way of centering us back into our bodies.

More than that, painting—because it is such a flexible and adaptable form of art—gives us unparalleled freedom to express what we are feeling. Through colors, forms, lines, even fabrics, we can tap into our deepest emotions and thoughts; we can access our very source. Given this opportunity, we unburden our spirits and are freed to express ourselves. Painting is an excellent way of tapping into our spirituality and nurturing our spiritual selves.

You will start with more simple painting exercises that will remind you of your connection to spirituality. You'll begin to feel a quickening and a sense of aliveness that you may not have felt in a long time. Even if you are an artist, the exercises presented here can rekindle the spark of passion that may be missing from your painting experiences. No matter what your level of experience, you will feel a spiritual connection with your first experiment in chapter 1.

Although many of my students come to painting later in life, I discovered it relatively early, and by the time I was sixteen, I was teaching art to a group of World War II veterans. I loved that experience so much that later I earned a BFA in art education and began teaching high school art in New York. I eventually left the public schools and began painting full time. I later opened an art gallery and art school and taught students of all ages. During the whole time I taught painting, I continued to travel and paint and take workshops with different artists and teachers.

Finally, after about thirty years of teaching art and selling my paintings all over the country, I was drawn to the practice of yoga, which I studied for several years. My yoga practice so transformed me that I became a certified yoga instructor. Combining yoga and painting seemed a natural thing to do. I discovered that the two combined have an almost magical ability to bring us closer to our spirituality. I still combine yoga and painting in my workshops and seminars, including many of the exercises and art projects in this book. Many of my students who take my yoga and painting workshops express gratitude that they have found their calling and a way to connect with spirit. I hope that by pondering the spiritual themes and trying the body-oriented exercises and art projects in this book, you will discover this connection to your own spirit for yourself.

ART AND SPIRIT

Humans have had the urge to paint since the dawn of time. The paintings in the Lascaux cave in France, estimated to be about seventeen thousand years old by paleontologists, are vivid evidence of this ancient urge. Although most of us will never view these paintings firsthand, as the caves were closed in 1963 to prevent deterioration, we can witness their beauty by looking at photographs on the Internet and in books.

The walls of the Lascaux cave, discovered in 1940 by teenagers, are covered with beautiful paintings of deer, bison, and horses. This cave is considered to be the pinnacle of Paleolithic cave art, with figures entirely covering the upper reaches of the walls and the first third of the vaulted ceiling. Many hidden chambers and vaults within the Lascaux cave show herds of animals running together. One noteworthy chamber, called the shaft of the dead man, portrays an encounter between a dead man and a bison, with a fleeing rhinoceros on the left. There is also a painting of an assegai—a slender spear.

The realistic renderings of these animals can evoke a sense of wonder. They reveal the eternal irrepressible urge of humans to portray their lives. What inspired these drawings and paintings? What urge compelled these early artists to paint images using only crude torches to illuminate their work? I believe that these early paintings expressed the hunters' connection to the mysteries of spirit. They must have felt the power of the animals that they depended on for sustenance and expressed their awe through painting. Whatever their original intent was, the paintings convey a spiritual power and energy that anyone can feel.

This power and energy has flowed from paintings ever since. Go into any art museum and you will behold walls filled with paintings that exalt the sacred and the sublime. Great paintings can touch our souls deeply and connect us to spirit.

What is spirit? In Sanskrit, spirit is called *prana* or life force. In Chinese, the term for spirit is *chi*, the energy that flows through all things. Many people perceive spirit as God, nature, a higher power, or all that is. Spirit can be a calling, a quickening of the heart, a deep knowing within us of what is essentially unknowable. I, myself, believe spirit can be understood as the eternal side of life. Most of us have glimpsed it from time to time, often unexpectedly—seeing something inexpressibly profound in the last remaining rays of sunlight on a field or in the graceful flight of a hawk. Whatever form these encounters take, we recognize them as heightened moments in time, and we know they have added a special dimension to our usual experience of life. Glimpsing the eternal is a transcendent experience—brief, perhaps, but very real.

You, too, can touch and express spirit through the practice of making paintings. Even if you don't make great art that will one day hang in a museum, you can make *important* art that has profound personal meaning for you and possibly for others who see it. The practices in this book will help you to open channels to power, spirit, and creativity.

SEEING THROUGH ARTISTS' EYES

What we paint affects us, certainly, but our work can also touch other people. Artists throughout time have helped us to see things in a new way, opening up a new window on reality, a new worldview. One artist that has touched me deeply with his unique vision is Edward Hopper, known for his paintings of life in America during the 1930s and 1940s. He depicted lonely "nighthawks" drinking coffee in diners, old houses, and lonely, alienated people enduring isolation, despair, and boredom.

Such dark images may seem an unlikely way to connect to the spirit. But something in Hopper's work inspired me. I felt a deep connection to the lonely images he painted. It seemed that I knew those deserted streets in a very personal way. I could sense the feeling of early morning that he portrayed by painting long shadows on the pavement in a small city. And the people he painted were familiar to me. His way of creating sharp contrasts and strong sunlight made me feel sad, lonely, and yet enlivened.

In an attempt to portray life as a clearly as he did, I studied his oil paintings in museums. I loved the way he used light and dark to define form. His skillfully blended oil paints give solidity and weight to his figures. He used juicy oil paint with beautiful nuances of color that show the brush strokes. I could see how he mixed his colors, and I borrowed ideas from him.

I began my own personal painting exploration of the old buildings in the historic part of town where I lived and began documenting the faded glory of these places: the old hotels, abandoned houses, and even the stray dogs that lived inside garbage cans and under discarded furniture. I even bought an old rooming house with a room that had been a Hungarian restaurant and converted it into an art gallery, in which I displayed and sold my artwork for many years.

Whatever it was about Hopper's work—the skill of his brush, his uncanny understanding of light and shadow—it opened up a place inside me that allowed me to express my spirituality through the act of painting. Hopper inspired me to travel, document the American scene, learn how to paint in both watercolor and oils, and fulfill my calling as a painter.

I'm sure you have experienced inspiration, insight, and even spiritual awareness by looking at artwork. Perhaps the essential role of the artist is to portray the qualities in our lives that are inexpressible in ways other than through lines, colors, textures, and shapes. In the same way that artists provide a new way to perceive life, we too can create artwork that provides a new way of seeing for ourselves. Once we discover what lies hidden within us, we can more easily access it and express it in ways that inspire others and ourselves.

BEGINNER'S MIND

In some ways, I will be asking you, whatever your experience with painting, to continually become a novice once again through what Japanese Zen priest Shunryu Suzuki Roshi calls "beginner's mind." Beginner's mind is just that—a state of mind that is continually refreshed and emptied. With a mind that is empty of preconceptions and fixed ways of doing things, there is room to discover something new!

Through the practice of beginner's mind, we can approach the exercises in this book with an open and curious mind, not needing to know the outcome, or even how to do it. With this mind, as Suzuki Roshi says, there are many possibilities. Even if you are an artist with painting experience, you can still approach this book with beginner's mind. With this attitude, every art project will be new and fresh. This book is not for experts, rather it is for anyone who wants to try new things.

When the French painter Paul Cézanne declared, "The day is coming when a single carrot, freshly observed, will set off a revolution," he alludes to the power of beginner's mind to turn the world upside down. Seeing something with totally innocent eyes can be revolutionary!

As you explore the exercises in each chapter, keep returning to beginner's-mind consciousness, whether you are a novice or experienced painter. Try to empty your mind and keep yourself open to each moment. Sometimes beginner's mind feels uncomfortable, because you may feel like you know absolutely nothing. It's OK to feel this way. Bringing that attitude to each chapter offers you the experience of being like an empty vessel, ready to be filled to the brim with breath, experiences, emotions, color, and paint—glorious paint! Remember to return again and again to this state of mind.

THE JOURNEY BEGINS

Our ultimate destination is to find our connection with spirit by making art. We will start right where we are, and together we will go step by step into the unknown. Focusing on our breath and our bodies will help prepare us. Our memories, life experiences, and intuition will guide us. The tools of painting—brushes, color, paper—will get us there.

We might even say that there is no concrete destination, no real place to arrive at; there is only our journey, our moment-to-moment experience. We are pilgrims on a path returning to our creative and spiritual center. This is wonderfully freeing news: Since there is no actual place to arrive at, we needn't worry about the results of our experimentation with art materials. Our only job is to enjoy the ride. Our job is to explore, observe, play, and savor the experience.

Before embarking on your journey of discovery and adventure, you will need to prepare for the trip. There are three main things you will need to do in preparation: prepare a space in your home where you can do the yoga-inspired body exercises; prepare a painting studio; and become familiar with your options for purchasing art materials.

PREPARING YOUR YOGA SPACE

First, reflect on ways to create a comfortable area for the practice of the body-centered experiences. If you already have a space set aside in your home for meditation, stretching, or exercise, that space might work fine. If not, consider setting aside a room or a corner of a room where you will not be bothered. This space should be quiet and feel inviting and cozy, but it does not have to be elaborate. You'll need a couch or sturdy chair, a yoga mat or rug (an area rug is fine), and a tape recorder (optional).

You may want to have an altar. On it you could put photos of loved ones or spiritual figures and mementos, or meaningful souvenirs, such as seashells, crystals, stones, or stuffed animals. You could put pillows and a blanket on the couch, so you can relax after your exercises. Everything you put in this space should help you to feel safe, cozy, and nurtured.

PREPARING YOUR ART STUDIO

You will also need a place to do the art projects. This can be the same space as your yoga space, but it does not have to be.

Your art studio should have a large table and a sink and should be well ventilated. It should also have some shelves to store your supplies, including plastic containers and jars, and a place to store your works in progress and your finished creations. This room should be comfortable and private and conducive to your growth. The studio will become your sanctuary and temple—a sacred space that is yours alone in which to explore your spiritual world and creativity. This room will support your creative reawakening. Create a space that suits your needs. Have fun choosing items to enhance the nurturing aspect of this room.

DISCOVERING THE AWESOME WORLD OF ART MATERIALS

Each chapter in this book contains a list of suggested supplies you will need for each project.

The world is full of art supply stores, and there are discount art supply stores that you can order from online. Many art supplies are readily available in hardware stores, such as wet or dry sandpaper, masking tape, chip brushes, turpentine, and sponges. Other materials are available in popular craft stores and office supply stores.

You will notice in the list of materials that some of them are optional. For example, if you are exploring pastels, you don't need a huge set, which may be expensive. You can start with a small inexpensive set and see if you like that medium. If you do, there's plenty of time to buy more.

One of my favorite things to do is to shop for art supplies. I like making up my little list, going to the store, and wandering up and down the aisles, taking in all the wonderful colors and imagining all the possibilities contained in the brushes, canvases, pastels, paints, and pens that I see. Let your shopping for supplies be part of the wonder of your painting experience. Take your time. Choose items that catch your eye. Let yourself be like a kid in a candy shop as you admire the gorgeous variety of watercolors, pastels, and papers. Let your spirit open up. Who knows, you might even find inspiration for a new project right there in the store! And don't be afraid to ask a salesperson for help if you're not sure what to buy.

THE PATH FORWARD

The chapters in this book all have the same format: They begin with a discussion of a spiritual theme, then present a body-centered experience to help you flow more easily into the painting experience, and finally give an in-depth exploration of an art project.

Chapter 1 ponders the question, "Whatever happened to our natural creativity?" Intentional breathing exercises are used to calm the mind and bring energy to the body. In the art project, you will playfully experiment with oil pastels, or Cray-Pas. The purpose is to remind you of the fun you had as a child coloring with crayons.

Chapter 2 explores the power of drawing to help us see what is before our eyes in different but complementary ways and ponder what "realistic" really means. In the body-centered experience, you will use a yoga strap to "draw" in the air with your legs, which opens the hip flexors. Three simple art projects explore using the drawing media of pencil, vine charcoal, and brush and ink.

Sometimes the things our souls truly long for become covered by everyday worries and responsibilities. In chapter 3, you will learn to get in touch with your deep yearnings, first through some gentle spinal movements designed to open the breath and increase a sense of expansion in the body, and then by painting whimsical pictures with watercolors.

Chapter 4 will help you reclaim your authentic personal power and artistic vision in the face of external and internal critical voices. Through your body-centered experience of *dirgha pranayama*, or three-part breath, you will cleanse the lungs and center the mind. Then through the painting process of resist, you will combine oil pastels and watercolors into a magical experience that will put you in touch with your innate creativity and artistic wisdom.

In chapter 5 you will see how practicing the concept known as *witness consciousness* can help you step back from your thoughts and emotions— which often include worries or judgments about your artwork and your life—to see things more clearly. Meditative breathing will encourage this frame of mind. You will then use soft pastels to draw a still life.

In chapter 6 you will examine the theme of going with the flow of life. The body-centered experience uses simple joint movements to release synovial fluid and warm the body, developing flexibility in the body and in the mind. You will put this flexibility to use by learning how to liquefy soft pastels to create an underpainting, over which more pastels can be added to create some strikingly beautiful pictures.

In chapter 7 we will delve more deeply into the concept of beginner's mind. Our body-centered experience is called *seagull breath*, in which you use your arms to increase lung capacity and develop an open mind. The painting experience is the ancient Indonesian art of batik, using wax and dye to create paintings on fabric.

Chapter 8 introduces the medium of collage, the process of arranging and pasting cut and torn papers to express a theme, as a method to help uncover long-hidden dreams and aspirations. You will also use a yogic breathing technique called *alternate nostril breathing*, which balances the hemispheres of the brain and encourages tranquility.

In chapter 9 the idea espoused by Swami Kripalu that "self-observation without judgment is the highest spiritual practice" is explored. In the body-centered experience, you will be guided in a face massage that will prepare you for the painting project. You will then use pastels to paint a self-portrait as you behold your face, and yourself, with nonjudgment and compassion.

In chapter 10 you will learn to nurture your intuition, first through a breathing experience called *breath of joy*, and then by painting a human figure using water-soluble oil paint.

In chapter 11, you will consider the power that stories have in our lives. The body-centered experience will include an eye exercise that will stretch the muscles in the eye and symbolically help you to see more clearly into yourself. The final painting project will be an autobiography to help you investigate ways that you might reinterpret one of the limiting stories in your life in a more empowering way. The form the autobiography takes is up to you and can be a work in progress because of its scope.

My students and I have painted using all the art materials presented in the book. We have also practiced the body-centered experiences, which prepare us for the painting practices. My hope is that the ideas and projects in this book will encourage you to express yourself creatively and joyfully.

1 REMEMBERING YOUR ARTIST SELF

PLAYFUL EXPERIMENTATION WITH OIL PASTELS

Out beyond ideas of wrong doing and right doing,
there is a field. I'll meet you there.
When the soul lies down in that grass,
the world is too full to talk about.
Ideas, language, even the phrase "each other"
do not make any sense.

—RUMI

I have always loved to paint. Artists paint for different reasons: We love color, we want to express the images we have in our minds or what we see around us, or we simply want to immerse ourselves in the beauty of creating something that comes from our hearts. Sometimes we just adore the delicious feeling of spreading the creamy colors on the page and seeing something emerge from nothing. Many of us paint because it offers us a time to be alone with ourselves without having to interact with anyone else and to simply follow our intuition.

Some of us embraced painting early in our lives because it felt like the perfect way to express what was inside of us. Others of us discovered painting more recently, perhaps chancing upon it while we were coloring with a child or after seeing a notice for a painting class in a catalog.

The urge to create is inherent in all of us and is an essential component of the human spirit. It's a fundamental drive. Even Genesis 1:1 says, "In the beginning, God *created* the heavens and the earth." We find the theme of creation in every religion and civilization, expressed in some form of myth that explains how the world began. Perhaps since we are all part of the spark of creation, we all wish to create our own world and express our experiences of being alive. Painting is an excellent way of doing this.

In this chapter you will explore the source of creativity and the sheer joy and expressiveness of painting. You will use intentional breathing to help still your body and mind, and then you will work with wildly vivid oil pastels, one of my favorite media, and simply color, draw, and play around with them to remind yourself that art, at its core, is *fun*.

PAINTING BEGAN AS PLAY

I believe that when we were very young we were absolutely swimming in a realm of pure potential, of wonder and possibility. We were open, flowing, and creative and totally connected to our spirit, the part of us that is one with everything. Have you ever noticed how babies can go from smiling, to crying, to smiling again in a matter of seconds? They are connected to a pure energy source that, I believe, is also the source of our creativity.

I happened to discover the power of painting when I was quite young. I remember discovering that I could play with color and just make it up as I went along. From the very beginning, my painting was all about joy and goofing around and letting my imagination run wild. When I look back on those days, I also see that it was an outlet for me, a safe way for me to express my feelings during a sometimes turbulent and anxious childhood. I was absorbed in the simple act of trying out different colors and inventing shapes and patterns and even imaginary animals.

Today, I still love to play with color, allowing the beauty of the moment guide me from stroke to stroke. When I am painting, I am in a world that is very familiar to me, not because I've been painting for so many years, but because I seem to know that territory from another time or space. It's not that I know what I'm doing, but more that it feels right for me to be doing this. Very often, I don't know exactly where the painting is going, but I know I'll find out as I do the dance of painting. When we can give ourselves the space to play with the paint, we are much freer to listen to our intuition and to enjoy our painting experience.

FROM PLAY TO GETTING IT RIGHT

But for many of us, myself included, somewhere along the way, painting became less playful and more something to "get right." If you've been painting for years like me, you probably remember a time when you experienced a similar shift. If you are first encountering painting, you might suffer from judgmental thoughts, such as, "I can't paint anything worthwhile," or "My paintings don't look realistic at all!"

When we are actually in the act of painting, we may put a stroke on the paper or canvas and immediately regret or doubt the color we chose. "That blue is much too dark," we think to ourselves. "I've ruined the painting." Sometimes a critical, uninvited comment from a friend or relative can plant seeds of doubt in our minds, and sometimes even prevent us from pursuing our love of painting. Experienced artists and beginners alike will encounter those times when they wonder why they even chose to paint. We may begin to doubt our abilities and become discouraged. Oftentimes, we get so discouraged that we just stop entirely.

Spanish painter Pablo Picasso once said, "All children are artists. The problem is how to remain an artist once he grows up." What happens to us when we leave our childhood? It seems that so much of our spontaneity and creativity wanes, and we lose touch with a tender part of ourselves. Sometimes as adults, we hear a whisper from the past, a voice that calls us to return to the artist who lives within us. The question that Picasso poses is a spiritual one, and this chapter will ponder his question and seek ways

Remembering Your Artist Self

for us to return to our innocence, exuberance, and full spiritual and creative expression.

Not everyone experiences damaging critical voices while growing up. Some of us get enough encouragement to give us confidence in expressing ourselves artistically, perhaps going on to become writers, painters, or dancers. Others of us have had harsh experiences that discouraged us, and sometimes these criticisms follow us into other areas of our lives, and even as adults we may become increasingly rigid in our ideas of what is safe to express in our lives. Mostly, we do what we think we are good at and avoid what we believe we are not good at. The judging, critical, and often misguided voices from our past stay with us and are very powerful. These voices take up residence in our heads and influence our lives in profound ways. For that reason, remembering your playful artist self can help soften those critical voices in every area of life.

My own transition began when I started being recognized as an artist. I was shy and insecure when I was young, but I was lucky enough to have had teachers in my early years who encouraged me and drew me out of my shell. My fifth-grade teacher, Mrs. Gerstman, asked me to paint scenery for a play about the Lincoln-Douglas debate. While everyone else did math, I painted at the front of the room with tempera paints on large paper, making scenery and backdrops. This teacher is partly responsible for the encouraging voices I often hear in my head when I'm painting, cheering me on.

But the flip side of that approval was that I began to feel compelled not just to paint but to be a good artist. This meant producing works of art that would earn me more praise—in other words, to get it right. This same impulse followed me into adulthood when I made the decision to become a professional artist and art teacher. Talk about pressure to get it right! My very livelihood depended on my artwork pleasing other people so that they would open their wallets and shell out tens, hundreds, or even thousands of dollars. Depending so heavily on giving other people what they wanted did not encourage the playful side of art-making.

Yet, I never lost touch with the urge to return to the simplicity and playfulness of the artist within, the part of me who does not earn her living from being an artist. When I am free to express myself authentically, I do not worry about making the artwork look acceptable to anyone but myself. I yearn to go that deeply into painting.

You may have many different messages in your head, some encouraging and others not. You may be an artist of some kind, a painter or sculptor, but nevertheless still occasionally be plagued by discouraging voices. Whatever your experience, this is a chance to just play around with paints and explore them in any way that calls to you.

PAINTING OUR WAY BEYOND RIGHT AND WRONG

In the poem that begins this chapter, the mystic Sufi poet Rumi tells us of a place that is beyond all our concepts of right, wrong, and separation. Painting can be both a method of recapturing your native creativity and also a path to Rumi's wonderful field of spiritual growth. He suggests that when our soul enters this place, we know that words are insufficient to describe our experience. This world that Rumi alludes to is a field that is safe and free of the illusion that we are separate from our source. He invites us to lie down in this field that is devoid of criticism, comparison, and evaluation of others and ourselves. You may remember a time when you were young, before you learned about right and wrong, when you felt this joy and boundless freedom. I believe that we are all yearning to return to this field.

My students tell me that when they are painting they get a glimpse of this field beyond "right doing and wrong doing" that Rumi refers to. When they break through the barrier of fear and doubt and plunge into a painting, they are renewed. One woman told me that she experiences happiness and peace when she is painting in nature. Most of my students report that they love the beauty of the colors and the way they feel when they are moving their hand over the page.

WHY OIL PASTELS?

The first project in this book uses oil pastels. I've chosen oil pastels because they are juicy and colorful. They are easy, simple, and direct and can

instantly transport you to a place of childlike excitement. Just looking at their brilliant colors gets your heart beating a little faster, and then choosing your first color is like digging into your first box of forty-eight crayons.

These oil pastels, sometimes known as Cray-Pas, are waxy sticks of color that are often covered with a paper wrapper for easy handling. They are fun to use because they come in bright colors and go on the paper easily. You can color with them like crayons, but because of their waxy texture, you can blend them and combine colors. For example, you can paint a layer of yellow on the paper, cover over it with a red oil pastel, and mix these colors to make orange.

These sticks of waxy, brilliant color can help lead you right into the field that is far beyond right doing and wrong doing. They are excellent for just messing around on the paper, exploring forms and colors and anything else that comes to mind. They bring out the artist in you because they lend themselves to the sheer enjoyment of moving them around on the page. You can move beyond the limiting concepts of right and wrong. Your practice using this medium can lead you to release judgments about your ability and even to let go of the need to achieve or accomplish anything. The finished painting will be one that simply evolves from a place of ease and comfort and playfulness. Oil pastels can help you remember the artist within.

GETTING READY

So that you can easily transition from the body-centered experience into the art project, gather your oil pastels and other materials into your studio space before you begin practicing the breathing exercises.

Let's Connect with Our Body and Breath

The first step toward returning to the field beyond right and wrong is to begin to get in touch with your body and to calm your mind, which may be scattered, doubtful, or skeptical. By practicing a preparatory breathing exercise, you will be able to calm your mind and let go of some of its chatter and commentary. Focusing on your breathing will also bring more oxygen to the bloodstream and the brain, thus bringing more energy into your body.

Our first experience focuses on breathing in a conscious way to help you tune in to your body. We all know how to breathe, but here you will actually spend time exploring the breath. By focusing on the breath with your eyes closed, you shut out visual distractions, helping to quiet your mind and release judgmental thoughts.

When I am jittery or nervous, I breathe consciously because I know that I will feel better after focusing on my breathing for a while. Before teaching a yoga class, or even while I am painting, I often sit on my cushion, close my eyes, and just go inside myself and breathe. When I close my eyes, all I am aware of is how my body feels and the rhythm of my breathing.

Remember to practice beginner's mind by approaching the next exercise with openness and curiosity. Let yourself go fully into the breathing experience; after it is over you'll be ready to paint with oil pastels.

Note: I encourage you to read each section through, before practicing, to familiarize yourself with each process. Do each exercise separately and savor each one fully. You may also use a tape recorder and read each section, and then play it back to yourself and follow your own instructions.

1. Sit on a chair or couch and close your eyes or, if you prefer, keep your eyes open with a soft gaze. Settle into your chair and feel it support your body. Simply relax until your thoughts become less active and your body begins to feel more relaxed.

2. Bring your full attention to your breath. Become aware of where you feel your breath in your body. Can you feel it flowing in and out of your nostrils? If not, notice where you do feel the breath. Feel your belly and chest expand and contract. If you notice that you are tensing your belly, relax it. If you notice any tight or contracted place in your body, visualize yourself sending the breath to that place and feel it relax.

3. When you feel calm and safe, bring to mind the image of yourself as a small child who is coloring or painting. See yourself alone and engaged in this activity. Take as much time as you need to thoroughly feel and notice everything about this scene—the sights, sounds, air temperature, and any details. How do you feel as you observe yourself as a child engaged in this creative activity? Continue to feel your breath flowing in and out of your body.

4. As you visualize yourself as a child, are you aware of any voices or feelings that are preventing you from thoroughly enjoying this activity? If so, what are they saying? Simply observe your thoughts without judging them. Continue breathing smoothly and steadily, watching the breath as it enters and leaves your body. If there are no distractions, simply notice this.

5. Think of the breath as your anchor with your creator self, the one who expresses what is truly in your heart and soul. Stay connected with your experience and your breathing. Let your thoughts encompass everything without suppressing them. Simply observe your memories and thoughts.

6. When you feel ready, open your eyes. Stay in touch with all your feelings and thoughts and take some time to adjust to your current surroundings.

LET'S PAINT!

Our first art project is to explore oil pastels to find out how they work and to reacquaint you with the simple, joyous act of choosing colors and creating lines, shapes, and forms on a page.

This is also an opportunity to observe your emotions as you work with the oil pastels, including any distracting or negative thoughts you may have uncovered during the body-centered experience. You don't have to do anything with those thoughts, just notice them.

As psychotherapist Carl Jung once said, "The creation of something new is not accomplished by the intellect but by the play instinct acting from inner necessity. The creative mind plays with the objects it loves." Take some time to fall in love with the oil pastels, enjoying them for their unique qualities. Focus on what you like about them.

Many Colors, Many Possibilities

THINGS YOU WILL NEED

- *Box of oil pastels, at least 12 colors (more colors are better)*

- *Drawing pad of sturdy paper, at least 11 by 14 inches*

- *Colored construction paper, a few sheets*

- *Knife or other sharp object*

Sunburst by Anne Katzeff
(see color insert).

Give yourself over to the experience of blending the colors, coloring one on top of another and seeing how they combine. Feel the creaminess of the pastels, and see how they react to the paper. As you color, release control of your arm and hand, allowing the oil pastels to guide you into your experiments.

1. Open your box of oil pastels. Take some time just to admire and savor the colors.

2. Choose your favorite color first, the most beautiful one in the box.

3. Open your drawing pad, and make a mark on the first page. Draw any line or shape that comes naturally to you. Don't think too much; just put down the lines that come to you spontaneously. Trust that your hand will make the right movement and marks.

4. Begin to draw other shapes. Draw whatever comes into your mind, such as a sun, some flowers, a house, or even a person—and remember that you can't go wrong no matter what you draw.

5. Focus on the texture of the oil pastel and how it feels on the paper. Does it go on easily, or is it hard to apply? Do you find yourself worrying if you are doing it wrong? If so, whose voice is that? Does it reflect your own true beliefs? If you like working with oil pastels, what about it feels good?

6. Choose another color that attracts you and continue to explore by making any marks, shapes, letters, or even words that come to mind. Make marks that feel instinctive, like scribbles, curlicues, zigzag lines, or circles. Put one color directly on top of another and see if they blend.

7. Explore all the colors that are attractive to you until you don't feel like adding anything more. Do critical voices have anything to say? If so, what response can you give from your authentic, creative self? What do you love the most about your painting?

8. Here are some additional suggestions for exploring oil pastels:

THE PAINTING PATH

- Try making a rainbow, beginning with yellow, the lightest color. Then add orange, red, violet, blue, and green. Blend the colors together until you like the way it looks.

- Try peeling the paper off an oil-pastel stick and draw holding the stick on its side, making broad strokes on your paper.

- Explore working on colored construction paper as well as white paper. Try using very bright colors on dark paper. How is that experience different?

- Make a scratchboard drawing: Draw assorted shapes in a variety of sizes and colors and completely cover the paper. Completely cover over those colors using a black oil pastel. Then, using the tip of a knife or other sharp object, cut into the black top coating. Make lines such as scribbles, circles, and shapes as you expose the colors underneath. Explore this method for a while, and see what you invent.

Reflections

When you are finished drawing, put down your pad, close your eyes, return your attention to your breath, and sit quietly for a moment or two. When you feel ready, turn to a new page in your pad and write about the previous experience and consider what was challenging, fun, surprising, painful, or peaceful. What did you learn about yourself from this exercise? Look at your drawing and notice what you feel and think about it. If you are unsure of what to write, use the following phrases as starting points. Remember that there is no right or wrong answer or experience to have in this process. All your awareness and emotions are necessary for retrieving your natural flow of self-expression.

I am now aware of feeling …

When I was little I loved to …

If I could do it, I would start …

As an adult, I really am …

What stops me from doing what I love is …

I know that I can always …

Whether you are a seasoned painter, a novice, or just curious about painting, by opening yourself up to the experiences in the following chapters, you can learn to let go of self-doubt and fear and learn to dance and play with colors. It's a little like walking by the ocean's edge as the waves come onto the shore. You dip your toes into the water and feel the coolness travel up your legs. You lift your pant legs up to keep them dry, but eventually give in to the delight of the ocean waves, as you let them soak your clothing. Finally, you just can't resist jumping in!

2 WHAT'S REAL?

LOOKING BENEATH THE
SURFACE WITH DRAWING

*All that we see or seem
is but a dream within a dream.*
—EDGAR ALLEN POE

We are all born with the desire and ability to draw. As children, we drew spontaneously all the time with crayons, pencils, pens, and markers—sometimes in places we weren't supposed to! When we draw as adults, even if we haven't drawn for a long time, we can find that spontaneity as easily as if we had never stopped. Drawing is something that we feel deeply in our souls. As the French painter Henri Matisse once wrote, "Drawing is not an exercise of particular dexterity, but above all a means of expressing intimate feelings and moods."

But why a chapter on drawing in a book on painting? There are several reasons. First, when you are painting, you are always using drawing skills whether you are aware of it or not, no matter what painting technique you are using. Taking some time now to practice some fundamental drawing techniques will serve as a solid foundation for later projects.

Second, drawing can bring peace and tranquility and be a means to connect with a powerful inner force. The act of drawing is a brave act. It takes courage to create a new reality, to fashion something from nothing, to face the blank page. It can also be playful, keeping you from taking yourself too seriously, even transporting you back to childhood. As you experiment with pencil, vine charcoal, and brush and ink, you may be reminded of times when you used to draw when you were younger, when it was a simple joy. I love to draw, and by the end of this chapter, I hope you will rediscover the joys of drawing, too.

Finally, drawing can give you unique insights into understanding reality itself. Sometimes, you may judge your drawing on how "realistic" it is, but accurate representation is only one component of drawing. Indeed, even how realistic something is depends largely on your point of view. As the Edgar Allen Poe quote that begins this chapter points out, the nature of reality is slippery, and what is real to one person may not be real to another. Even what seems real to you now may not seem so real later on.

This chapter's body-centered experience will let you "draw" with your legs in the air, and then you will explore a variety of drawing techniques using pencil, vine charcoal, and finally ink-and-water washes.

CAPTURING THE ESSENCE

I love what cartoonist and illustrator of Bugs Bunny, Chuck Jones, said, "The whole essence of good drawing—and of good thinking, perhaps—is to work a subject down to the simplest form possible and still have it believable for what it is meant to be." A drawing can capture the essence of something through accurate draftsmanship, but it can also express the spirit of something abstractly, using bold shapes and patterns rather than duplicating details.

I remember myself at age six, a ballet student at Miss Anna's School of Dance, drawing pictures of dancers' legs, ballet slippers, and pastel-colored tutus. I was intrigued by the form of a dancer's legs especially the shape of the calf muscle. I drew the bulge of the muscle, experimenting with line to describe the shape and shading to express strength and solidity. I made drawing after drawing of her legs, trying to both convey what they looked like and express the wonder and delight I felt watching her legs move gracefully as she spun around the room.

Years later, I still try to look past the surface and express the spirit of what I'm drawing. One of my passions is traveling and visiting ancient ruins. I always carry a sketchpad and pencil wherever I go. A few years ago I traveled to Mexico and encountered a young Lacandon Indian man. This Mayan tribe fled deep into the Yucatan jungle to avoid capture during the Spanish conquest. With less than seven hundred surviving members, these gentle souls still wear traditional white handwoven tunics, and their jet black hair hangs down their backs. When they make a rare appearance in a Mexican Internet café, often barefoot, they are a strange anachronism. When I drew this Lacandon man, my pen explored the contours of his Mayan profile, the sharply cut bangs on his forehead, and the way his tunic flowed in heavy folds onto the tile floor. I remember observing my subject as he sat patiently, my pencil gliding over the surface of the paper, expressing the lines, shadows, and energy of the man. I tried to emphasize the salient features that made my subject unique as a man, but I also wanted to convey

Lacandon Indian, Palenque, Mexico, 1993 by Linda Novick (a travel journal page).

his gentle spirit. Drawing enabled me to do that simply and directly, without the distractions of color or other more complex painting techniques.

But the process is different for everybody. The Indian philosopher Krishnamurti once wrote, "Truth is a pathless land." Although he happened to be speaking in a philosophical context, I think his words nicely capture the essence of drawing, which is—anything goes. The important thing is to observe your subject as deeply as possible, discover what you want to express about it, and start drawing. Work from your own heart. As you let go of concepts of "how to draw," you will learn to draw.

BUT IS IT REALISTIC?

The most common complaint I hear from my students when they complete a drawing is, "It doesn't look realistic!" Perhaps you feel the same way about things that you draw. I can certainly understand that feeling. In the earliest drawings that I can recall doing, I was so concerned about making my subject look realistic that I used carbon paper to trace the profile of a beautiful woman whom I wanted to draw.

Later on, I ventured into freehand drawing, but still labored to make my drawings as realistic as possible. I recently found a yellowed, torn crayon drawing of mine from first grade showing Pilgrims and Indians sitting down to Thanksgiving dinner. I admired the details I had included, such as the Indian holding a hatchet, the cooked turkey, the Pilgrims' costumes, and the perspective of the table.

Where did I get the idea that drawings are *supposed* to look realistic? Where did any of us get it? In fact, this phantom idea has stood in the way of many people who love to draw. As a result, even though drawing is so accessible, expressive, and fun, many people are afraid to put pencil to paper because they think they won't be able to make things look realistic enough.

But just what does "realistic" mean, anyway? A detailed drawing in a medical textbook may look realistic to a student, but to Vincent van Gogh, whose images are heartfelt and very expressive, it may appear cold and lifeless and therefore not realistic at all. The awkward stick figures drawn by a child may look realistic to the child, but not to his or her parent. A map of the world or the solar system drawn in the fifteenth century might have been perfectly realistic then, but look quaint or even primitive to modern eyes. I get a good chuckle when I see the ancient maps that depict dragons and monsters rising out of the oceans at the "end of the earth."

DRAWING EXPRESSES DEPTHS OF REALITY

Drawing is much more than achieving a realistic result. Instead, drawing is a process of exploration and discovery. This drawing process investigates observable data—the shape of things, how the light falls on them—but equally important, it also opens up concepts and images from our imagination, or what we see in our mind's eye. It helps us see beneath the surface of things. In drawing, not only does the artist seek to represent a kind of reality through the use of lines and shapes, he or she also represents a deeper kind of reality, one that is personal and meaningful to the artist.

Vincent van Gogh once wrote to his brother Theo, "What is drawing? It is working oneself through an invisible iron wall that seems to stand between what one feels and what one can do." This statement conveys the idea that drawing for van Gogh was a means to express his deepest emotions about life, a reality beyond even what he saw. We also sense how he struggled to improve his drawing skills and express his soul. He often found himself stifled by frustration and self-doubt, unable to even work on his drawings. In another letter to Theo, he says, "In spite of everything I shall rise again: I will take up my pencil, which I have forsaken in my great discouragement, and I will go on with my drawing."

Cancun, Mexico, 1993 by Linda Novick (a travel journal page).

We can all relate to van Gogh's frustration and feelings of inadequacy. There are times in which we all find ourselves unable to accomplish or express adequately what we see in our minds and feel in our souls. When we sit down to draw and face the blank page, we often experience discouraging internal dialogues and self-doubt.

At such times, it may help to remember that drawing, for all its power, can also be very simple and even goofy. The Swiss artist Paul Klee wrote, "A line is a dot that went for a walk," and "A drawing is simply a line going for a walk." These words evoke the image of little dots and lines going on their merry way, climbing mountains or bouncing around making their marks on a piece of paper. Klee made whimsical watercolors and drawings of funny shapes, colors, and lines and little animals, especially birds and fish. They don't look realistic in the conventional sense, but they aren't meant to. They have a different purpose—to make you smile.

Your drawing skills will naturally improve the more you draw, so don't let "getting better" become your focus. Instead, give yourself permission to be a beginner at drawing, and let the process of drawing open up your imagination and relax your view of how you think things are or should be. Let drawing take you to that field that is beyond right and wrong. Drawing is much like living, something to observe, enjoy, and experience.

DRAWING IS AS OLD AS THE HILLS

Drawing is one of the earliest forms of visual expression that we know of. We have discovered cave drawings in France that date back to approximately 15,000 BCE. These beautiful and sensitive drawings express the power and grace of a variety of large animals. In 1995, Australian archaeologists uncovered a four thousand-year-old Aboriginal rock art site in the Wollemi National Park, near Sydney. Previously hidden by inhospitable geography, the site contains more than two hundred well-preserved drawings executed in charcoal, white pipe clay, and yellow and red ochre. Over twelve layers of images have been superimposed, one upon the other, depicting birds, lizards, kangaroos wallabies, geckoes and life-sized, delicately drawn eagles. (See the World Socialist website, www.wsws.org, for Susan Allen's article on the Wollemi Rock Art, published August 5, 2003.)

Drawing has also long been used for other types of communication. In pictograms, a form of writing, drawings represent ideas. Pictograms were used in many early cultures, such as Native American in the American Southwest. In ancient Mesopotamia (modern-day Iraq), pictograms date back to at least 3400 BCE, when the Sumerians used them to record agricultural and social transactions.

Yet for such an ancient art form, the basic tools and materials for drawing have hardly changed since prehistoric times. They include sticks, brushes of wood or bone and animal hair, charcoal, paint, ink from berries, chalk, and virtually anything that will make a line. When we draw today using very similar materials, we are connecting in a physical way to the many artists who have gone before us. We are participating in an activity that is almost as old as humanity itself.

I once took a class in which we carved our own pens from pieces of bamboo, and then drew with them. When I drew with this pen, at first it felt clumsy, but as I practiced with it, I sensed my connection to ancient Chinese artists who used pens made from the same material. I also felt connected to artists in the Middle Ages who used similar materials to illustrate illuminated manuscripts. I liked the strong strokes that I could get using this reed pen that I had made by myself. I feel the same way when I draw with charcoal, which has been used for over thirty thousand years as a drawing material and a pigment for painting. When we explore our world using the very same materials used by the ancient peoples, we can't help but feel a kinship and connection with them. In the same way they did, we seek to understand and express reality as we know it.

As you explore the drawing projects, let yourself become immersed in the experience of using these materials. Give in to the experience of feeling the textures in your fingers and the applying of them to paper. Sense the burned wood in the charcoal and the ground pigments in the ink. Connect to the universal energy contained in the materials you are using, and perhaps even to the people who first used them. You may even sense the wonder of the cave dweller who discovered that he could draw with the charcoal that cooked his meal the night before. Feel the connection between you and every artist who ever used brush and ink or pencil.

WHY THREE ART PROJECTS?

I have included three different drawing exercises in this chapter so that you can sample pencils, charcoal, and brush and ink, along with the different effects that different drawing techniques can accomplish. I think my favorite material to use in this chapter is brush and ink, perhaps because I love painting so much. I enjoy using the thick, rich black ink and experiencing the depth and weight of it. I love the way I can dilute the ink, using varying amounts of water to make lighter washes. Probably because I can be looser, brush and ink is a favorite drawing medium of mine.

Trying different media allows you to really feel the physical sensations each has to offer—how the pencil feels in your hand, how the lead scratches off onto the surface of the paper, or how the charcoal is smooth and cool in your fingers. These feelings become absorbed into your physical experience and stay with you even as you move on to new projects.

These drawing projects also demonstrate the power of black and white as a form of expression. Using only black and white allows you to focus more carefully on the beauty and subtlety of the range of grays. As you use shading, you become sensitive to different degrees of lightness and darkness—called value—and how you can achieve a variety of values using only a few drawing materials. Drawing with water and ink mixed in a variety of proportions—called washes—offers you the opportunity to focus on dramatic compositions and strong surface patterns, without the distraction of color. Confronting the object of your drawing in this straightforward manner helps you see the object in a new way.

Let go of having to do a good job during the drawing exercises. Instead, use beginner's mind and think of yourself as a kindergarten child who comes to school to play with drawing materials. Approach things without any expectations, with a mind that is open to all possibilities.

GETTING READY

To prepare for the art project, we will "draw" in the air with our feet and legs in our yoga-inspired body experience. Before you move to the body-centered experience, however, gather together all the materials you will need for the art project. Also, make sure to cover your drawing surface because the charcoal and ink projects can become messy.

 ## LET'S CONNECT WITH OUR BODY AND BREATH

The following body experiences are called tie-yoga movements because they use a strap (such as a necktie, although a length of rope or a belt will work, too) to help guide your legs into the proper positions. You can use the tie to support your legs so that they rest in it, as in a sling or a hammock.

I use these in many of my classes. They are designed to lubricate the hip flexors by charging these joints with synovial fluid. This natural lubricant contained in all the joints of the body is readily available to be released whenever we move our joints in a repetitive way. In addition to increasing fluidity within the hip joints, these movements stretch and lengthen the muscles in the legs, in particular the hamstrings and the quadriceps.

These exercises create a sense of freedom and expansiveness in the hips, pelvis, legs, waist, and lower back. We store a lot of tension in these areas of the body, and these exercises are very effective in releasing blocked energy and opening up a channel of positive flowing life force, called *prana* in Sanskrit. I have also chosen this exercise because it mimics the act of drawing. When I lead this experience in my classes, I direct my students to dip their toes into an imaginary bottle of ink and explore the space around the body. This is also the perfect antidote for those who struggle to create realistic drawings, always want to get things right, or get mad when they make what they perceive as mistakes. Drawing In the air with your legs makes it impossible to take yourself too seriously.

Note: It's OK to refer to the book and the illustrations for help as you perform the movements. If you don't want to refer to the book, record the instructions on tape and play them back to yourself, or have someone read the instructions to you. Or simply read these instructions over a few times until you are familiar with the exercises and can do them without assistance. If you have difficulty getting down onto or up from the floor, feel free to perform the exercises seated on a sturdy chair or couch. The results will be the same.

Tie-Yoga Movement 1

Choose a tie, such as an old necktie, a belt, or a strap. Lie on your back with your tie at your side. Relax your whole body. Allow your breath to be smooth and steady. Feel the support of the floor beneath you.

1. Bend your left leg and place your left foot on the floor close to your buttocks. This left leg will be an anchor, so keep it firmly on the floor.

2. Hold the ends of the tie, one end in each hand, so there is slack in the tie. Bend your right knee and lift your right foot into the air. Place the middle of the tie below your toes or on the ball of the foot, wherever it feels comfortable. Be sure your arms and elbows are relaxed with your shoulders on the floor.

3. Extend your right knee and stretch your right leg up toward the ceiling. Using the tie to help guide your leg, use your foot like a big crayon and draw an imaginary circle on the ceiling. Begin with a small circular movement. As your hip flexor feels more comfortable, increase the circle to the size of a watermelon, and then to the size of a hula hoop.

4. Reverse the direction of the circle. Get a sense of using your leg to draw into the space over your body. Explore different-sized circles.

5. Drop the tie, bend your right knee, and lower your right leg. Interlace your fingers and use them to pull your right knee into your body. Apply gentle pressure. This movement releases and relaxes the muscles in the lower back. Breathe smoothly as you hug your bent knee to your chest. Remember that you can rest anytime you feel like it.

6. Now, place your right foot on the floor close to your buttocks. Using your right foot as an anchor, repeat this process with your left leg and foot.

7. When you have completed the movements with your left leg, gather both knees in your arms and gently pull your knees toward your chest, making your body into a little ball. Make circles with your knees in one direction, and then in the other direction.

8. As you circle your knees, press your lower back into the floor. You will feel a gentle massage on your sacrum as you circle your knees. Relax your legs and let your arms do the work. Finally, release your knees and lower your legs to the floor, one leg at a time.

9. Bring your arms out to rest at the sides of your body. Relax and let your arms and legs sink heavily into the floor. Simply breathe and experience what you are feeling.

THE PAINTING PATH

Tie-Yoga Movement 2

This movement is designed to stretch and lengthen the inner thigh muscles. It will also create a sense of openness in the hip area.

1. Bend both your legs and place both feet on the floor close to your buttocks. Lasso your right foot as you did before, but this time put both ends of the tie in your right hand.

2. Stretch your leg out and point your foot at the ceiling, then slowly lower your right leg out to your right side, moving it gradually toward the floor. Stop when you feel resistance, a stretch on the inside of your thigh. Do not go any further than is comfortable. Hold the leg out to the right side and allow the stretch to produce a feeling of openness in the hips. Breathe deeply and smoothly. When you are ready, let the leg come to the floor out in front of you.

3. Repeat this with your left leg. Remember to hold both ends of the tie in your left hand, and lower your leg to the left side of your body.

Tie-Yoga Movement 3

This movement will increase the sense of freedom in your legs and thighs as well as help limber up your legs. In addition, this movement simulates the feeling of drawing, as you are actually drawing with your legs in the air.

1. Lasso your right foot as before, keeping both ends of the tie in your right hand.

2. Move your right leg in broad, sweeping motions from one side of your body across to the other side. Pretend you are drawing

a rainbow with the right leg, back and forth. To make this movement easier, allow your body to roll onto your right hip as you lower your leg to the right, and roll onto the left hip as you lower your leg to the left. Move your leg from side to side two to four times, or as many times as feels comfortable.

3. Repeat this movement using your left leg, holding both ends of the tie in your left hand.

4. When you experience a sense of freedom and openness in your hips and your mind, hug both knees into your chest and rock gently from side to side.

Take a few minutes to rest and integrate your experience. What did you feel in your body? What thoughts came into your mind? Allow yourself time to become grounded in your body and integrate the experience. Whenever you are ready, slowly make your way to your studio and begin the art project.

LET'S DRAW!

Contour Line Drawing Using Pencil

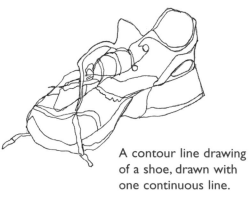

A contour line drawing of a shoe, drawn with one continuous line.

THINGS YOU WILL NEED

- *Several sheets of sturdy white paper, at least 11 by 14 inches (experiment with different textures)*

- *Interesting objects to draw (fruit, shoes, flowers, a ball, your hand)*

- *Pencil, number 2B or 3B (not HB)*

You make a contour line drawing by allowing your eyes to carefully follow the contours of an object and then reproducing them on paper. The fun part is that you are not allowed to lift your pencil off the paper as you draw: it is a continuous drawing composed of a single line. There is no shading, only a line that goes for a walk on your paper, for a long time. If not lifting your pencil sounds like it might be tricky, it can be; it requires some discipline to keep your pencil on your paper as you work. But if you remember to follow the rules, you will have fun, probably a few laughs, and end up with an interesting picture.

In addition, this technique gives your drawing a spontaneous, unstudied look, even slightly crazy and a little out of proportion—a perfect way to learn that making something look realistic is often only a minor concern when creating art. This technique will make you laugh, both while you are doing it and when you look at the resulting drawing!

Be sure to use a 2B or 3B pencil to draw with because the lead is dark and soft and flows onto the paper easily. Stay away from HB pencils, as the "H" stands for hard, and hard lead is difficult to slide around the page. Also make sure the object you choose to draw interests you, such as your own face (using a mirror), your hand (perhaps holding an object), a sneaker with untied laces, a backpack, a high-heeled shoe, or a sleeping cat or dog

1. Look at the object you've chosen for a long time until you start to notice some pertinent information about it. Look at its shape and think about filling up the whole page with this object. Imagine where you'd like to start. For example, if you're drawing your face, you might begin at the eyes or the top of the head.

2. Place your pencil on the paper and begin to move it slowly. Imagine that you are a bug walking on the surface of this object with your little insect legs. Being so small, you can't walk too fast, so move the pencil over the paper slowly, as if to caress each part of your object.

3. Continue to imagine yourself as a bug exploring the contours and shapes of your object. When it goes up, you go up. When

What's Real?

it curves to the left, so do you. Also, remember to go inside the object, veer off the beaten path by exploring not just the contour, but its interior. If you draw your hand, be sure to include the lines in the knuckles, and the folds in the skin.

4. You can stop moving the pencil to take time to observe your object, but don't lift the pencil from the paper! If you need to get from one side of the object to the other side, create a bridge with a lighter line, by lessening the weight you apply to the pencil. This will give you a less obvious line while keeping the line continuously moving.

5. As you draw, think about how it feels to draw that continuous line. What is your experience? Do you feel anxious about getting it right? Do you want to fix every mistake? You may notice that the proportions of your drawing are funny and the object looks distorted, even goofy. Don't worry about it, it will look distorted and goofy. Remember—realistic is in the eye of the beholder. It's OK to laugh at your own drawing!

6. You will know that your drawing is complete when it seems to come to life with details. When you are finished, lift your pencil off the paper.

Take a step back and look at your drawing. Does it look like a child drew it? If so, great! That means you let this experience have a spontaneity and sense of freedom and whimsy that is at the heart of art. Anytime you find yourself overwhelmed with a great urge to get something right—whether a piece of art, a project at work, or anything else—you can do a contour line drawing to loosen your mind. It's almost impossible to be serious when you are doing a contour line drawing.

Reflections

Use the following questions to ponder the drawing experience you just had. You can write your thoughts right alongside your contour drawing, if you wish. Don't worry about getting the answers "right."

What reality can contour line convey to the viewer?

How does practicing this technique relate to your life in general?

What has changed for you since doing this drawing?

What did you find most challenging about this experience?

Creating Solid Objects with Shading Using Vine Charcoal

THINGS YOU WILL NEED

- *Several sheets of sturdy white paper, at least 11 by 14 inches (experiment with different textures)*

- *Interesting objects to draw (a pitcher, fruit, a statue, flowers, a wine bottle)*

- *Pencil, number 2B or 3B (not HB)*

- *Vine charcoal*

- *Kneaded eraser*

- *White tablecloth and table*

- *Desk lamp or other source of direct light*

Still Life with Fruit and Chinese Pot by Linda Novick.

Drawing a still life is a terrific way to explore shading because the objects are not going to move: you can take a break and return to the project any time you choose. Working with charcoal and eraser is a wonderful way to discover how using light and dark can create the illusion of solid objects—a step toward making a drawing look more realistic.

This project has two parts: first is setting the stage and arranging your objects. In this part, you create a reality that will be your subject. It is fun because you can choose objects that are meaningful to you or that have interesting shapes.

In the second part, you will explore the reality you composed and arranged. Let yourself become thoroughly curious about the relationships of objects, shadows, light, and dark. Look for patterns within the arrangements of objects. This project explores form in a different way from contour drawing, concentrating on light and dark shapes, rather than pure line.

1. Choose interestingly shaped objects for your still life, such as apples, which are spherical; bananas, which are cylindrical; or a box of tissues, which is rectangular. Or choose objects that may have special meaning for you. I enjoy drawing garlic, gourds, small sculptures, pears, and bottles of Chianti.

Step 2: Arrange your still life objects on a white tablecloth (see the finished drawing on p. 39).

2. Cover a table with a white tablecloth and arrange your objects in a way that you find pleasing. (The tablecloth will help you see shadows more clearly.)

3. Once you've arranged your objects, place a light source, such as a desk lamp, on one side of the objects. Make sure the lamp creates areas of light and dark on the object and that it casts shadows on the tablecloth.

4. Take some time to notice how the light hits the objects. Where are the lightest parts of the objects? Where are the darkest? How does the light

influence your perception of the objects—which surfaces are near and which are far away? Look for the shadows on the tablecloth.

5. When you are ready to draw, sketch the objects by first focusing on their contours and shapes. Hold the charcoal at a slight angle, allowing the line to have a soft fuzzy look. Keep your arm relaxed and apply the charcoal to your paper gently. Keep your lines light and airy.

6. When you have the contours of the objects sketched, draw in the shapes of the shadows you see. (You will shade them in during the next step.)

7. When you have drawn the contours of the shadows you see, use light, feathery strokes to shade in the shadows. Press harder or lighter according to how dark or light the shadows are.

8. When you have drawn the objects and their shadows, remove the plastic from around your kneaded eraser and knead it as if you were playing with Silly Putty until it becomes soft and malleable. Form it into a point and erase any lines you've made that you want to remove, or gently lift off layers of charcoal, lightening the shading. These subtle refinements can really bring the drawing to life. When the eraser gets dirty, clean it by massaging and kneading it and blending the charcoal back into the ball of the eraser. Keep a damp rag available to clean your hands occasionally.

Continue to enhance your still life gradually by erasing, drawing, and blending with your finger. When you don't know what else to do with your picture, you're done!

Reflections

When you are finished, answer any or all of the following questions in this book or your notebook.

What did you learn about reality from using the charcoal and eraser?

How did light and shadow influence your drawing experience?

What was most fun about doing this drawing?

What was most challenging about this project?

Using Brush and Ink to Explore Values

Preparing for the Show by Linda Novick.

THINGS YOU WILL NEED

- *Several sheets of sturdy white paper, at least 11 by 14 inches (experiment with different textures)*

- *Dynamic black-and-white photograph or newspaper clipping showing athletes, dancers, or animals in action*

- *Pencil*

- *Small watercolor brush, number 10 or 12, made of hair or synthetic hair*

- *Jar of India ink*

- *Plastic container for water*

- *Small plastic palette with indentations for ink (you can also use a Styrofoam egg container)*

- *Roll of paper towels*

The purpose of this exercise is to learn to draw with a brush and mix washes of different values, and to explore interesting compositions (the way shapes are arranged on the page). You will create a wash drawing that replicates the values and movement in a black-and-white photograph.

Note: The best kind of photo to work from is one with strong action and movement that contains a variety of values from light to dark. It should be one that calls to you and compels you to explore its shapes and dynamic rhythms.

Values are subtle gradations from black to white. They can be made using pencil, charcoal, ink, or black crayon, as well as ink washes. You can express the white value by leaving the blank paper white, without putting an ink wash over it. When you are finished, if the blank paper looks too shockingly white, simply put a very light wash over it to "soften" the effect so it appears to blend in with the rest of the values in your wash drawing.

This photo shows movement and strong values of light and dark between the two horses and the girls' clothing.

This exercise will help you let go of your perception of objects as fixed, immutable, solid, and separate. Using the fluid medium of ink wash, you can begin to explore breaking the boundaries that seem to exist in the real world. As you use your brush to "wash in" reality, you symbolically let go of minute details and see things with a broader view.

This is going to be a very loose drawing, and you need not replicate the actual action of the figures or even make them look like fig-ures. Instead, look for the *prana* or life force in this photograph, and see if you can represent it by using a variety of graduated washes.

Step 1: Use a pencil to block out the general shapes.

1. Use a pencil to block out the general shapes. Don't try to be realistic: instead, divide the page into simplified, geometric shapes that represent the movement in the photo. Notice the direction that the subjects' arms and legs are moving in and include lines that indicate that movement.

2. After you've sketched the shapes on the white page, analyze the values that you see in your action photograph. Where is the absolute darkest value? It should be almost black or at least very dark gray. Where is the lightest value? Is it pure white, or a very light shade of gray?

Step 3: Use your pencil to shade in the shapes you've drawn.

3. Use your pencil to shade in the shapes you have just drawn. Press harder with your pencil to get a darker value and lift the pressure to achieve a lighter value. Leave the paper white where it appears to be white. Don't be afraid to go very dark in the areas that appear to be black.

4. Pour a tiny amount of ink into the compartments of your palette or egg container. Dilute each dot of ink by adding a bit more water to each segment of your container, lightening each value as you proceed, until you have a very light wash that has hardly any ink in it at all. Prepare as many different values as your picture requires.

5. Using a brush, apply the washes to your drawing according to the values in the photograph. Go right over the pencil sketch you made before, using the values you made with pencil as a blueprint for applying the washes from darkest to lightest. Aim to convey the energy, the essence, and the *prana* of the photograph, using shapes and contrast to convey action and dynamism. Clean your brush in clear water often to keep the values of the washes on your palette distinct. Explore loosening up and letting go of "getting it right." Use beginner's mind, and just see what happens without needing to control it too much. See my finished piece on p. 42 for an example.

When you are finished with the drawing, see if you've captured the movement and action contained in the photo. Observe the variety of values you've achieved in your work. It's not realistic, but is that important? Sometimes an abstract drawing, such as the one you've created, is much more powerful than a stiffly copied imitation of a subject. Notice what you like about your drawing.

As you admire your wash drawing, notice if you feel nervous, doubtful, or even wonder if you have made a mistake. Just notice those thoughts. This exercise can help you let go of perfectionism. You have not made any mistakes, rather you have shifted into a new reality and expanded your drawing skills. In the words of editor and writer Elbert Hubbard, "The greatest mistake you can make in life is to be continually fearing you will make one."

Put your wash drawing aside to dry, and take a moment to sit down and close your eyes. Return your attention to your breathing, and sit quietly observing your breath for a minute or two. Notice your feelings and thoughts, and let them be just as they are. Let all the visions and thoughts simply swirl around your head. Take time to relax and breathe, experiencing everything you are aware of.

Reflections

Write down your thoughts about what you have just experienced. Write in this book or in a notebook. Answer any or all of the following questions. Fill in the spaces in the following sentences about your experience. Feel free to write more if you want to.

What did you learn about reality from these projects?

What is the most liberating thing about these projects?

Which of the three projects was most realistic in your mind?

Which was least realistic?

When I was using the washes I ...

I found it challenging to ...

After the exercises I ...

Now I know I don't have to ...

GETTING IN TOUCH

DISCOVERING WHAT WE REALLY WANT
WITH WATERCOLORS

The breeze at dawn has secrets to tell you.
Don't go back to sleep.
You must ask for what you really want.
Don't go back to sleep.

—RUMI

I fell in love with watercolor when I was six years old. I was in the Brooklyn Museum where I saw the bold and expressive watercolor paintings of John Singer Sargent and Winslow Homer. I remember gazing at those paintings feeling joy, admiration, and a deep soul-excitement. I remember especially one of Homer's images, painted in the Bahamas, depicting dark-green palm fronds set against sparkling white houses, accented by bright red hibiscus flowers, and framed by a turquoise ocean. Homer conveyed the feeling of sunlight in the tropics with a few quick strokes of brilliant color. I was enveloped in the moment. It was a spiritual experience for me, and I knew deep in my soul that I wanted to be able to do the same thing that Winslow Homer had done—I wanted to be a painter. That day set the trajectory for my life.

I was fortunate enough to discover so early in my life what my body and soul yearned for. In today's world, it's not always so easy to know this.

As the pace of life in our world accelerates and technology spirals out of control, many of us find ourselves racing faster and faster just to keep up. And most of us know, on some level, that this is a mistake, that the faster we move through our lives, the more we miss. The more we do, the less we are able to savor each experience. Although, thanks to technology, we are more connected than ever before, we are often left at the end of the day with a feeling of isolation and a lack of fulfillment. We know all these things, and yet we very rarely make the effort to step out of the mad race, slow down, and discover just what it is that we, in our souls, truly long for. Maybe we think we don't have the time to do that, or that it will be too hard. Maybe we simply don't know how to do it.

In Mary Oliver's poem "Wild Geese," she reminds us that "you only have to let the soft animal of your body love what it loves." There is a gentle permissiveness about this. We don't have to chase after things to discover if we want them. In fact, it's just the opposite. Slowing down eliminates distractions, brings you into the present moment, and allows what your soul truly longs for to become apparent—like me at age six in the Brooklyn Museum.

We will explore this ourselves through a yoga experience designed to warm up our spine, bring increased energy to our body, and nurture creativity in our minds. We will also experiment with watercolor painting, including color mixing and painting spontaneously from our imagination.

DON'T UNDERESTIMATE THE POWER OF TOUCH

Entertainer Gypsy Rose Lee once said, "Anything worth doing is worth doing slowly." I totally agree with that statement, and I'll bet you do too. But alas, most of us are traveling far too quickly while hardly getting anywhere. I sometimes catch myself walking quickly to my car, going to the ATM quickly, hurriedly returning e-mails and generally speeding around. I guess I am getting things done, but what a frantic pace!

Recently I decided to slow things down a little and began tuning in to what I used to love to do. I started spending time at the library browsing. I also started going to the movies by myself, arriving early, getting popcorn, and watching the previews, advertisements, and finally the movie—simply luxuriating. In addition, I spend lots of time in bed reading and then falling asleep. These are simple, ordinary activities, but they are important to me, and they help me slow down and tune in to the "soft animal of my body."

We can all make a mental commitment to slow down and do a few favorite things that we have neglected. When we slow down, we can more easily listen to our inner urges, which are often masked by our frenetic movement through life.

On a more fundamental level, I think the real problem we face in our day of personal digital assistants, MP3 players, laptops, and cell phones is the loss of touch—both literally and figuratively. In the early days of telephone communication, a real operator would connect you with the party you were calling, which certainly added a human touch to the process. When you called a friend, you spoke to a real person most of the time, not an answering machine with a tinny recorded voice. We even wrote letters by hand on beautiful stationery or cheap, rough paper, and eagerly checked the mail every day for a response in the form of an envelope with a colorful stamp in the corner. These were sensory activities and real interaction with real people in real time.

Today's communication is often merely the cold transmission of data, devoid of the human touch. Many of us are busy faxing forms, answering e-mails, and following up on minutiae, but without becoming truly involved in any of it. We suffer through phone prompts and being put on hold. What's missing are the heart connections that we used to have when things were slower and less sophisticated.

Writer Susan Sontag laments the loss of actual objects that help connect us to one another: "Fewer and fewer Americans possess objects that have a patina, old furniture, grandparent's pots and pans, the used things warm with generations of human touch, essential to a human landscape. Instead, we have our paper phantoms, transistorized landscapes." Technology removed the human touch from our lives.

It is important to reconnect with simple objects that are organic and connected to the energy of humans and the earth itself. I have a hand-stitched, color-stained canvas holder for my watercolor brushes that goes with me on all my travels. My paints are made from pigment ground from materials found in the earth, and some of my paper is handmade by artists who create their own individual sheets, one at a time. The tools of the painter have the human touch, and by using them we too become more human.

Painting offers an opportunity to recapture some of those old ways. You literally get to touch things—beautiful colors, smooth paper, wet paints, slick brushes. And as an expression of yourself, you are inserting something of the human touch back into the world. Painting also forces you to slow down. It gives you a chance to put things on hold, to take time to be with yourself and tune in to the "soft animal of your body" to discover, or rediscover, what you love.

WHY WATERCOLORS?

I have discovered in my classes that watercolors in particular lend themselves to being in the moment. They are slippery and a little wild. They are extremely flexible, capable of producing fresh, brilliant colors when used with very little water, or pale, subtle colors when mixed with lots of water. The transparency of the paint allows the white of the paper to shine through, lending a luminosity to the colors of any shade. Because watercolors are very wet, they do not have the precision of a pencil point or even a crayon. In fact, they have a mind of their own—they are unpredictable, elusive, and magical. You have to let them do their thing. For this reason, watercolors are the perfect art medium for encouraging you to let  go of control, stop rushing, slow down, and enter fully into the delightful present moment of creation where your soul has room to stretch.

This really works. Many people have come to my classes from high-powered, fast-paced, often unrewarding jobs. They are often disconnected from themselves and from those around them. And yet something in them compels them to step out of the race for a week. They take the time to slow down, get in touch with their bodies through watercolors, and by the end of the retreat, they often share with the rest of the class that something inside them changed—they discovered they really didn't want to be in that high-powered, fast-paced job. They want something else for their lives. One woman who took my program recently fell so much in love with watercolors that she quit her job! She now paints part-time and works part-time.

LIQUID COLOR

One of the best qualities of watercolors is their versatility. By using a big brush, you can cover large areas of your paper with a bold, colorful wash, just as we did in chapter 2 with a wash of ink and water. But you can also use a small, delicate brush to create detailed strokes of color.

Two American watercolor artists whose works show the versatility of the medium are John Marin and Edward Hopper. Both men were born in the late-1800s and died during the mid-1900s, and their work reflects a slower time in America life. Hopper was born in Nyack, New York, and Marin in Rutherford, New Jersey. They both expressed a fiercely individual kind of painting whose styles differed greatly from each other.

Hopper's watercolors are eerily realistic depictions of life that emphasize lonely cities, illuminated by bright sunlight that casts long shadows, intimating the quiet languor of early morning and late afternoon. His realism is evidenced by careful attention to detail as well as defined forms using highly contrasting values.

Marin's paintings are expressionistic, using exaggeration of color and form to create an emotional effect. He painted the dynamic energy of the Maine Coast and Taos, New Mexico, using techniques he borrowed from Cubism, showing a landscape fragmented with a few powerful zigzag strokes, often employing angular abstract forms to enclose the composition.

WATERCOLOR HAS MANY POSSIBILITIES

We also benefit from the versatility of watercolors. There are limitless combinations of colors to create as well as happy accidents that occur when using watercolors. You can use them loosely, which means you don't have to try hard or force them. You can let them do their own thing by gently guiding them along with your brush. Just as you cannot control a bead of mercury in your hand or an excited Springer spaniel (nor would you want to), you can't make watercolors do exactly what you want them to do. Slow down when you try them, and let them reveal their magic to you.

There is an energy contained in your brush, and you can express the gesture of things by using your brush in the right way. You can use your brush to create expressive strokes of color, such as lines, curlicues, dots, and circles. With your brush strokes, express the energy of grass growing or rain falling.

For me, a brush has its own special *prana*, and it flows out of the bristles when you paint. Let yourself tune in to the *prana* in your brush, and let it guide you. Use your brush as an extension of your arm, and let your own *prana* flow out. Relax your arm, relax your brush, and let go and paint.

In addition to the brush, there are three basic techniques available to you when you paint with watercolors.

WASH

Watercolor washes are terrific because they can be applied in big bold strokes, using a large brush to cover a large part of the paper. They can also be used with a smaller brush to paint tiny patches of color. The thing to remember when you make a watercolor wash is to use enough water. The wash should create a bright, luminous area of color, because the beauty of watercolors is revealed in their flowing, radiant quality.

WET INTO WET

Another watercolor technique, which kids really love (and you will, too), is wet into wet. First, you wet your paper by applying a wash of clear water. Then you load your brush with a beautiful color and apply it to the moistened paper. This technique releases a burst of color that spreads in rivulets throughout the moistened page. You can add a second color and watch the colors bleed together.

You can also begin with a wash of one color, and then introduce a second color into that wash before it dries. For example, you can apply a bright yellow wash on the paper and then add a blob of red paint. The result will be an unpredictable explosion of red as it enters the yellow wash, creating an effect like fireworks! I say unpredictable, because it really is. You never know exactly how a stroke will come out, especially with wet into wet. Many artists use this technique when painting a rainy day landscape or a tumultuous sky preceding a storm. It is also great when you just want to mess around and enjoy playing with color.

DRY BRUSH

The third watercolor technique is called dry brush, in which you use very little water. Because of the lack of moisture, your strokes will appear textured and even pick up the grain of the paper. Artists often use dry brush on top of washes, once they have dried, to create the effects of grasses, bark on trees, and the grain in wood. It is the exact opposite of a wash, as there is very little feeling of the wetness and etherealness of watercolor. This technique works well if you enjoy being detailed, as you can create interesting textures using dry brush.

All these techniques are available to you as you work with watercolors. Use them to explore the field beyond right and wrong. Let them help you slow down and get in touch with what you love. Let their magical unpredictable ways encourage you to let go of the need to get things right. There is no way to get it wrong! Tap into the magic of the colors to bring yourself into a communion with your inner knowing. Find the sense of joy and connection with a slower way of being fully present in the moment. Allow the watercolors to touch you deeply on all levels.

GETTING READY

Since you will transition directly from the body-centered experience into the painting project, before continuing to the next section, gather up your materials, cover your painting table with newspaper, fill the plastic container with water, and generally get ready to move into painting.

LET'S CONNECT WITH OUR BODY AND BREATH

Your spine is one of the most important parts of your body, allowing you to stand erect and move and bend with great flexibility. The spinal column protects your spinal cord, the powerful bundle of nerves that runs from your brain and branches out into the rest of your body. When you move the spine in certain ways, you open up areas of the nervous system that may contain blocked energy. Since our thoughts are intricately connected with our bodies, releasing blocked energy will help release our creative energy. When the spine is open, the mind is more open, and this helps us express ourselves more freely and easily.

In my yoga classes, we open up our spines through a movement consisting of two stretches, often called cat stretch (or cat pose) and dog stretch (or dog pose) because they imitate the way cats and dogs arch their backs when they stretch. These stretches are best practiced on a rug, yoga mat, or a thick blanket spread on the floor. Some people find that doing this exercise in front of a mirror helps them attain the correct position.

Note: You may wish to read this exercise through once or twice before doing it so you don't have to refer back to the book. Or record the instructions on your tape recorder and play it to yourself. If you do record it, leave some pauses in the tape, to give you time to practice the movements.

If you have limited mobility or have difficulty getting onto the floor on your hands and knees, not to worry! I have included a modified version of these stretches that you can do while sitting on a chair or couch.

Cat and Dog Pose in Table Position

1. Get down on the floor on your hands and knees with your back flat, your spine parallel to the floor. This is called the table position. Place your hands directly under you shoulders with your fingers spread out like a fan, and place your knees directly

under your hips. Distribute your weight evenly between your knees and your hands.

2. Visualize your breath entering and leaving your body. Consciously elongate your spine by pressing your head away from your tailbone and your tailbone away from your head. If you are using a mirror, you can check the position of your back. Try to keep it parallel to the floor, but don't force or strain.

3. Bring your attention to your tailbone at the very bottom of your spinal column. Gently tilt your tailbone down and turn it under, and at the same time, let your head drop, tilting your chin toward your chest. Press your belly up into your spine and let your back take on a rounded, arched position. This is the cat pose. Hold it for a few seconds. What sensations does your body feel?

4. Now reverse this posture. Begin by tilting your tailbone up toward the ceiling, and let your belly drop toward the floor. Lift your chest and head toward the ceiling. Your back should be arched downward, exactly opposite of the cat pose. This is the dog pose.

5. Let your breath flow freely as you get a sense of this new position. What sensations does your body experience? Are they different from those you felt in the cat pose?

6. Repeat these movements, alternating slowly between the two poses. Become aware of your breath flowing in and out of your lungs. Which pose allows your lungs to expand with more freedom and ease?

7. Visualize a clean open space between each vertebra and imagine that you can send your breath there. With each inhalation, visualize your lungs expanding to accommodate more oxygen. With each exhalation, imagine that you are exhaling your tox-

ins or fears. Feel the luxurious stretches that your spine can make. Alternate between these two poses until your spine feels open and your mind feels calm and focused.

8. Slowly roll onto your back and use your arms to pull your knees into your belly and chest. Gently rock from side to side. Bring your full attention to your breathing and allow this focus to relax your body and your mind. Keep your head and neck on the floor as you rock from side to side; enjoy this gentle spinal massage. Rock in this way for one or two minutes.

After these movements, you may feel much more in touch with your body as well as your spirit. By moving the spine in alternate directions, you have freed up lots of energy—physical, mental, and creative. You will be in a receptive open state in which to flow into your watercolor project.

Seated Cat and Dog Pose

If you have difficulty getting onto or up from the floor, use these modified directions for cat and dog pose.

1. Sit comfortably on a couch or chair with your hands on your lap, palms down. Consciously elongate your spine by pressing the top of your head toward the ceiling. Simultaneously press your buttocks into the chair. You will begin to feel a sense of lengthening in your entire spine and neck.

2. Bring your attention to your breath. Breathe slowly and rhythmically, focusing on inhaling and exhaling fully. Allow your mind to slow down, and feel the weight of your body supported by the chair.

3. When you are ready, as you inhale lift your chin toward the ceiling and move your chest outward. Lean forward, stretching from the waist as you move your chest toward your thighs.

4. Next, press your tailbone toward the back of the chair. Press the top of your head backward in the direction of your tailbone and feel an arching of the spine. These actions move you into the dog stretch. Pause in this position and breathe calmly for a few seconds.

5. When you feel ready, reverse the direction of the spine. Slowly drop your head and let your chin move down toward your chest. Press the middle of your back into the chair and concentrate on moving your pelvis forward. Press your back into a rounded position. This is the cat pose.

6. Remain in this position for a few seconds, until you are ready to reverse the position and return to dog pose.

7. Alternate slowly between cat and dog stretches until you feel a sense of elongation in your spine. As you repeat these movements, practice slowing them down. How do you feel as you slow things down? Stay focused on your breathing. See if you can feel a sense of freedom and openness in your mind and body.

You may experience any number of things following your cat and dog stretches, including feeling relaxed, tired, focused, or energized. No matter what your experience is, it is part of the process of slowing down. Take your time before you begin to paint. There is no hurry.

Let's Paint!

The project that follows is an exploration of mixing watercolors. It is a way to develop spontaneity and self-trust. As you begin your painting exploration, remember the feeling of openness in your spine you achieved in the cat and dog stretches. Let the energy they released flow through you now. Continue to be aware of your breath. Whenever you find your mind wandering into the past or the future, bring your attention back to your breath and back to the project at hand. Invite yourself to try the following exercises with a light and playful attitude.

Exploring Your Watercolors

THINGS YOU WILL NEED

- *Set of watercolors with at least 8 pans of colors*

- *Number 14 watercolor brush made of synthetic or regular hair*

- *Number 10 watercolor brush made of synthetic or regular hair*

- *Drawing pad of white, sturdy paper, at least 11 by 14 inches*

- *Kitchen sponge*

- *Plastic container for water*

- *Roll of paper towels*

- *Newspaper to cover your worktable*

- *Several tubes of watercolors, including these colors: alizarin crimson, ultramarine blue, cadmium yellow, sap green, burnt sienna, and cobalt violet (optional)*

- *White plastic palette with a cover (optional)*

- *Pad of watercolor paper, at least 11 by 14 inches (optional)*

Keep lots of paper towels available to dry your brush whenever needed. Open your paints and slow down for a second as you admire the colors in your set. Connect with your feelings and your breath. Notice what you love about the colors. Which are your favorites? Get in touch with the beauty of this moment.

1. Open your watercolor set and use your brush to dab a bit of water onto each pan of paint. Be careful not to saturate the paint; use just enough water to moisten the paint and get it to soften and become creamy.

2. On your paper, paint a one-inch square of each color in your set of paints. You may paint the squares in a line, in a pattern, or placed randomly around the page. Label your colors with your pencil or with the brush. This will help you become familiar with the colors in your set and will serve as a reference to your colors.

3. Use the inside cover of your paint set as a mixing area to explore blending two colors to make a third. Dip your brush into red and place a glob of it in the mixing area. Clean your brush by swishing it in the water and then gently drying it on a paper towel or a moist sponge. Add a blob of blue paint to the red, and blend until you have created a new color. Paint a square of that new color on your paper, then label it with a name or a formula such as R + B = P (red + blue = purple).

4. Experiment by mixing other colors to create new ones. Some people like to clean the brush in water frequently, but others prefer to go directly from color to color without washing the brush. See which you prefer doing. Since blue and red are so much stronger and more dominant than yellow, however, you may wish to wash the brush before putting it into the yellow pan to keep the yellow clean.

5. Observe what your thought process is as you do this exercise. Does this project help you slow down? Does it seem easy for you? Remember that there is no one right way to mix colors. Trust your intuition as you practice this process. Do you like color mixing? Is it familiar to you? Are you slowing down and finding out what you love to do?

6. Some people are afraid to paint because they worry they will make mud. Try to mix a color that you call "mud." Label it "mud," and also write down the formula for how you created it so you can create it again. Maybe mud isn't such a horrible color after all. Get it out of your system! Mix all the muddy colors you can think of.

7. Notice if you are nervous, excited, frustrated, dissatisfied, or anything else you experience. If you have mixed colors before and this feels familiar to you, let yourself explore some new techniques for color mixing. What combination of colors have you never tried that you can try now? Slow down, take your

time, and come fully into the present moment. Get in touch with the beauty of the moment of color mixing.

8. Turn to a new page anytime you feel the urge. Think about trying some practice strokes and techniques that we mentioned before. Tune in to your breath and awareness of the present moment. Slow down and connect with your body and feel what you want to do next.

9. Try the wet-into-wet technique by using a number 14 brush to cover about one-third of your paper with a wash of clean water. Dry the brush on a paper towel. Dip it into a color you love, then plunge the color onto the moist paper. Watch what happens. Try this with some other colors. See what happens if you don't clean your brush between colors. Slow the process down and really look at the colors as they explode on the page.

10. Next, dip a number 10 watercolor brush into another color and paint some strokes. Try crazy shapes like dots, circles, lines, diagonal strokes, and squiggles. Paint them all over the page in any way you want. Try painting leaves, flowers, birds, trees, clouds—anything that comes to mind or flows from the brush.

11. When you don't feel like adding anything more, take a moment to return to your center by watching your breath. Sit down, and let this moment be real and vivid for you.

Reflections

Write down your thoughts about what you have just experienced. Write in this book or on your watercolor paper. You can use the following questions as a starting place.

What did you learn from this experimental session?

How did your creative energy manifest itself?

Can you see how this experience brought you into the present moment?

Did anything pull you away from the experience?

Painting from Memory and Imagination

I once heard a quote from the great portrait artist Alice Neel to the effect that painting from your memory and imagination helps you develop qualities of trust in your own abilities. It opens up a space inside you that reconnects you to your spirit.

The Cutest Dog in the World Not Counting Becky by Linda Novick (see color insert).

Oh, I Didn't Notice That the Canary Was Missing by Linda Novick (see color insert).

Children have no problem painting from their memories and imaginations, but sometimes I hesitate to paint from my memory and imagination because I am afraid that my painting won't look good enough. I prefer to paint from life, from direct observation of a scene or a person. But when I trust myself to use my imagination for inspiration, something emerges that often surprises and delights me, and often I laugh at my attempt because it looks so funny. Painting from my imagination helps me to lighten up.

This next exercise will help develop your intuition and self-trust. You might find that by trusting your imagination, you can learn to develop trust in other aspects of yourself.

1. Use a fresh piece of paper for this project. Close your eyes and picture a dog in your mind's eye. Let the image slowly become stronger and clearer in your mind.

2. Open your eyes and choose a color that matches the dog you just imagined. Without thinking too much, make a painting of this dog using any lines, brush strokes, or additional colors that you feel like using.

3. When you are done, wash your brush and prepare another sheet of clean paper.

4. Next, picture a cat in your mind. See it clearly, its shape, color, and size. Picture how it walks and moves. Trusting your vision, paint this cat on the second sheet of paper.

5. Do you find yourself judging the paintings, thinking they look silly or stupid? If so, remember that the process of painting can take you beyond the judging mind, beyond right and wrong. Anyway, we have all seen silly-looking cats and dogs. If you feel the need to slow down while you paint, feel free to put down the brush and do the body-centered exercises again.

6. Let yourself get into the spirit of the exercise. Be in the moment.

7. Next, put both paintings side by side. Scan your memory and imagination for images that pop into your mind of dogs and cats—big ones, small ones, striped ones, spotted ones, goofy ones. Add those images to your paintings. You can separate dogs from cats, or mix them all up.

8. Do your paintings look like a three-year-old did them? If they do, then you're on the right track! Give your cats and dogs names. Paint hats or other clothing on them. Give them jewelry. Give them a T-shirt with their name on it.

9. When you are done, stand back and enjoy your cats and dogs. Let your body love what it's done. If you choose to, you may want to do a few cat and dog postures to relax any tension that may have come into your body during the painting session.

Reflections

Take a moment to slow down, close your eyes, and tune in to your breath. Allow your thoughts and feelings to be exactly as they are. In the field beyond right and wrong, there is nothing that needs to be different than it is. When you feel ready, take time to answer any or all of these questions in this book or a notebook, and complete the phrases without thinking too much about them.

How does watercolor painting affect your sense of time?

What did you experience after practicing cat and dog stretches?

What qualities of watercolor do you enjoy most?

What is most challenging about painting from your imagination?

Watercolors make me feel …

I learned that I am really …

When I was painting I felt like …

The reason I move so quickly is …

If I had more time I would …

I'm afraid to slow down because …

4 YOUR CIRCLE OF POWER

REDISCOVERING YOUR AUTHENTIC VISION WITH RESIST

Power is strength and the ability to see
Yourself through your own eyes and not through the eyes of
  another.
It is being able to place a circle of power at your own feet
And not take power from someone else's circle.

—AGNES WHISTLING ELK

When we paint, we discover open avenues into places of profound personal power and insight. Painting in all its aspects allows our souls expression, free from the constraint of words or even logic. Engaging in art has the potential to give our imaginations free reign to express those feelings, beliefs, and personal truths we hold so close to our hearts.

Yet, many times it seems that even as we paint, especially when we are experimenting with new techniques or materials, we find ourselves shying away from expressing ourselves fully. We may self-edit, telling ourselves that our attempts are foolish. Other thoughts appear from nowhere and sabotage our creative efforts. Powerful voices inside us that may not actually belong to us tell us it's useless, we might as well give it up now before we embarrass ourselves, or worse.

Such experiences are common. My friend Debra calls this group of internal commentators the Committee. This group of judgmental naysayers analyzes everything she does. They seem bent on undermining her confidence and ability to grow as an artist and as a person. They are insidious, invading her creative space and robbing her of her unique, personal, and authentic artistic vision.

Almost all of us experience these voices at one time or another, or maybe all the time. Maybe you even have your own name for your version of the Committee. Yet, the more we paint, the more we may come to realize that although the Committee may never completely disappear, its criticisms do not have to control us. We have our own vision, and that's what we will begin to uncover in this chapter through a breathing technique called *dirgha pranayama*, or three-part breath, and a particularly playful form of painting called resist that combines oil pastels and watercolors.

CIRCLES OF POWER

The circle has a power and energy that has been recognized by cultures across the globe and throughout time. Everything moves in circles, including the rotation of the earth and the cyclical movements of our lives. The *enso*, a circle drawn with a single, broad brush stroke, is the Zen symbol of infinity, which represents enlightenment, encompassing the universe in an endless connected line.

The circle is also a symbol for completion, returning to our source and finding our way home. Native American culture has long revered the circle as the foundation of all creation. In the words of Black Elk, an Oglala Sioux holy man, "You have noticed that everything an Indian does is in a circle, and that is because the Power of the World always works in circles, and everything tries to be round…. The life of a man is a circle from childhood to death, and so it is in everything where power moves."

It is fitting that Agnes Whistling Elk, in the poem that opens this chapter, uses the image of a personal circle of power to represent the boundary between our own experiences, beliefs, and authentic vision and those of others. This is a remarkably powerful image, and one that we as artists can draw on when we encounter the strident voices of the Committee. Whistling Elk's phrase "Seeing yourself through your own eyes" implies that when we are inside our own circle of power, we can trust our own perceptions whether or not they line up with the perceptions of others. When we are within our own circle of power, we are free to find our own path and not rely on the directions others try to give us. This circle represents our ability to reclaim our most authentic self—who we really are, not who others have told us we are.

The problem arises for us when we step outside our circles of power and internalize the perspectives, judgments, and criticisms of others. (Perhaps we never knew we had such a circle in the first place.) When that happens, our authentic selves go into hiding, and we lose touch with our deepest wisdom. Our vision becomes lost. This is tragic, because we can truly create only from the center of our own circle, not from another's.

What can we do to recover our circles of power and lessen the power of the Committee's voices? How can we go about reclaiming our own authentic vision?

RECOGNIZE THE SOURCE

For most of us, the attitudes and opinions of our family played a uniquely potent role in forming our own ideas and beliefs—at least, what we often perceive to be our own ideas and beliefs—that very often carry on through our lives today. In fact, those voices from parents, siblings, relatives, and neighbors may be the very voices of the Committee that speak out when we begin to paint.

For example, if you were raised in a family that emphasized responsibility and respectability, art and artists may have been a focus of disdain. You may have heard a variety of myths about artists—what kind of people they were and what value they contributed (or failed to contribute) to society. Often these myths trivialized or denigrated their artistic abilities. Artists were strange, peculiar, and out of sync with the rest of the world.

Popular culture reinforces the image of the starving artist, the bohemian who lives in a garret with barely enough money to feed himself, railing against bourgeois convention, womanizing, binge-drinking, and teetering precariously between madness and excruciating genius.

Perhaps you heard a different message about artists. Or perhaps your family loved artists, but you somehow came to believe that you weren't good enough to be one. Whatever the specifics, the voices of the Committee received their attitudes and opinions from somewhere. And since the Committee is always in session, is it any wonder that these messages—which came from other people's circles of power, not our own—caused some of us to view our own artistic impulses with suspicion and distrust? We learned to curb our expressive impulses, just to make sure we fit in with everybody else.

I remember when, as a child, I first confessed interest in being an artist someday. My family reacted negatively, saying among other things that art wasn't a viable profession because, they said, "You can't make a living at it." Artists were foolish and, if anything, to be pitied for their naiveté and inability to hold productive nine-to-five jobs. I internalized those beliefs about artists, and even though I became one, I still wrestle with those beliefs, especially in lean financial times. At those times, the Committee rises up with words of discouragement, doubt, and self-reprisals, and I do feel out of sync with the rest of society with its focus on achievement and acquisition.

On the other hand, my inner artist knows that I have always been faithful to my authentic vision of life. I have loved walking in the rain, painting in remote villages, and trekking through the jungle in search of my dreams. I have chosen to live from my circle of power, choosing adventure, freedom, and expression over security, predictability, and in my mind, stagnation. I have followed my own path.

Realizing that the voices of the Committee don't actually belong to you is the first step in redrawing your own circle of power. The voices of doubt, judgment, even condemnation may remain, but knowing they come from outside your own circle allows you to begin listening for your own authentic voice.

REMEMBER THE GENUINE POWER OF ART

If the beliefs and opinions about artists that you have don't all genuinely belong to you, the next question might be what do *you* truly believe about art? For that, it might help to look at the data.

Think about a time that you visited an art museum. What was that experience like? Some of my students tell me that for them, entering a museum is like being transported to another world. They are swept up into the flow and energy of the artworks and discover new ways of looking at the world. Simply being in the presence of that art transforms them in fundamental ways.

Maybe you have been fortunate enough to see some of the world's truly sublime works of art, such as Monet's *Water Lilies*, or Michelangelo's Sistine Chapel or *David*, and realized in the presence of such work that nothing compares with the power of art to touch and convey the infinite. Even as those artists faced their own struggles—maybe not unlike the voices of practicality and reason that many of us struggle with—they found a way to bring their unique and authentic visions into the world.

Or maybe the very things about artists you were taught to disparage are the very qualities that, deep down, you admire: the artist's iconoclasm, independence, courage, and devotion to truth as he or she sees it; the trust in his or her true voice and vision. Is this compelling and refreshing for you? Are you inspired by the artist's ability to experience and express the agonizing valleys of life as well as the ecstatic peak experiences? Is that what, deep down, you are hoping to find when you paint?

In an inspiring poem by Rumi, he reminds us to "let the beauty we love be what we do. There are hundreds of ways to kneel and kiss the ground." These words attune our hearts with our authentic vision and remind us that creation is a holy act. Rumi encourages us to seek what we love and once having found it, to walk our chosen path with devotion.

When have you knelt to kiss the earth? What pursuits really called your name? In essence, what lights you up? Whatever it is, trust it. The Committee may say otherwise, but it is possible to remember the power of art in our lives.

REDRAW YOUR OWN CIRCLE OF POWER

You can learn to draw your own circle and cultivate your own wisdom regarding the worth and importance of the artistic, creative spirit. You can do this by taking your tools in hand and using them with conviction. You may be unsure at first, but with practice you will use them with power, grace, and confidence. You may not know what you are doing, but that doesn't matter. With the mind of a beginner, you have nothing to lose and no reputation to uphold. You do not need to be good at it; you need only recognize the innate yearning for self-expression, follow the calling, and see where it leads you. As dancer Martha Graham said, all that is necessary is to "keep the channel open."

One of my students said that she believed few people have an aptitude for art, and therefore, everyone else should stick to what they are good at. But why? Where is it written that only people with artistic talent should paint? And who is to be the judge of artistic talent anyway? If we stuck to only what we are good at—or what we thought we were good at—we would all miss out on many wonderful experiences. Author Henry Miller once wrote, "To paint is the thing ... not to turn out masterpieces. Even the Creator, in making his world, had to learn this lesson." In the act of creation, we are powerfully drawing our own circle of power. The more we paint, the more powerful our circle becomes.

This doesn't mean the Committee disbands. Author Eric Maisel said, "Creativity requires introspection, self-examination, and a willingness to take risks. Because of this, artists are perhaps more susceptible to self-doubt and despair than those who do not court the creative muses." But now we are engaging with the Committee on our own terms.

WHY RESIST?

Making a resist painting is a terrific way to experiment and make discoveries about colors, shapes, and images. Since there is no correct way to do resist, it can open a door to expression that is free of the constraints of other painting processes, such as oil painting. When using oil paints, we may feel the need to produce a great work of art, instead of letting our playful side take over.

I've designed an exercise using oil pastels and watercolor that can lead you into a childlike state of free-flowing invention and spontaneity. The first project involves pure experimentation, and the second involves a fun theme that draws upon your memory and imagination. Using your memory can be a strong tool in uncovering your powers of invention, and using your imagination helps reinforce the power of your own unique vision.

GETTING READY

Before beginning the body-centered experience that follows, prepare your studio for the resist projects by gathering your supplies, including paper, oil pastels, paints, and a container of water. By preparing ahead of time, you can flow from the breathing experience to the painting project without interruption, remaining focused from your breathing practice.

LET'S CONNECT WITH OUR BODY AND BREATH

The breathing technique known in Sanskrit as *dirgha pranayama*, also called the complete breath or the three-part breath, teaches us to fill all three regions of the lung, starting with the lower lungs, moving up to the middle thoracic region, and on into the upper clavicular region. This breath cleanses the lungs, calms the mind, and encourages concentration and creativity by supplying the brain with more oxygen. Learning to make use of our full lung capacity we increase the amount of *prana,* or life force, that flows through us and also expel more carbon dioxide. Through the practice of conscious, focused yogic breathing, we can begin to see more clearly into our thoughts and our motivations.

Note: Before you begin breathing, you may wish to read through the steps several times until you are familiar enough with the exercise so that you can do it without referring to the book. Alternatively, have a friend read the instructions to you as you practice, or read the instructions yourself into a tape recorder and play them back to yourself as you practice.

1. Sit on your chair or couch and plant both feet firmly on the floor. Close your eyes and relax your lips, face, shoulders, and belly. Feel the weight of your body settling deeper into the chair.

2. Lengthen your spine and sit up straight, but don't tense your body. Imagine that you are pressing the top of your head up to the sky. Lengthening the spine like this creates a free flow of energy in your body.

3. Inhale deeply and slowly through your nose to fill your lungs. Imagine filling the bottom of the lungs first, then the middle of your lungs in your midchest region, then the top of the lungs at the top of your chest. Feel your lungs expand like a balloon.

4. When you cannot take in any more air, expel the air little by little through your nose as if you were carefully emptying a pitcher of water into a slow, steady stream. Imagine the air at the top of your lungs leaving first, then the air in the middle of the lungs, then finally the air at the very bottom of your lungs.

5. Repeat the process, combining all the steps into one continuous flow. It may help you to place one hand on the upper chest and the other directly on the belly to feel how the body moves in and out. Concentrate on the expansion and contraction of your lungs.

6. Focus on the sensations of breathing and feel the breath in every part of your body. Do not force, strain, or try to inhale or exhale too quickly. With each in-breath, imagine taking in fresh, clean energy. With each out-breath, visualize releasing toxins and tension.

7. Repeat this process for up to five minutes. Notice the effects of this breath on your thoughts. You may notice that you feel more focused and relaxed. When you are ready, you may transition into the next exercise. Take your time transitioning to your painting project.

LET'S PAINT!

I have chosen the resist process because it is a great medium to explore creating your own circle of power and to "resist" any negative voices that might arise during your painting. It is a playful rather than a serious technique and can help you trust your own impulses and decisions.

The resist process combines two incompatible materials: wax and water. Just as a coat of wax on a car resists rain, oil pastel will resist the watercolor washes, which will slide right off, exposing the waxy crayon beneath. Depending on the thickness of the waxy material, you can control the amount of resistance you get.

Like Water off a Duck's Back

THINGS YOU WILL NEED

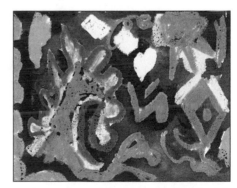

A resist experiment by Linda Novick (see color insert).

- *Box of oil pastels, at least 12 colors (more colors are better)*

- *Set of watercolors with at least 8 pans of assorted colors*

- *Number 14 watercolor brush*

- *1½-inch chip brush (from hardware store)*

- *Drawing pad of sturdy paper, at least 11 by 14 inches*

- *Plastic container for water*

- *Roll of paper towels*

- *Pad of student-grade watercolor paper, any size (optional)*

The first step is to experiment with the process of resist. Stay connected to your breath in a deep way, as this opens channels of creativity that may be blocked. By accessing these pathways you are reconnecting with your power.

1. Take a moment to look at the clean, white page in front of you. This page will be the place to use to reclaim your vision. Next, look at your box of oil pastels and choose a *light* color that appeals to you, such as yellow, orange, pink, or white.

2. Draw a shape on the page, any shape, anywhere. Because the theme of this chapter has to do with circles, you might consider drawing a circle or series of circles. Imagine as you make your mark that you are drawing a circle of power that claims your right to be creative and to follow your authentic voice.

3. Press down hard, and be sure to cover the paper well in the area you are working. If you do not press hard, the line will be too thin and will not resist the watercolor wash.

4. Continue adding more circles or any other shapes, such as triangles, wavy lines, flowers, trees, or suns. Follow your intuition. Use different colors, but stick to the lighter, brighter ones because they show up better when you paint over them with a dark watercolor wash. See the color insert for an illustration of the first part of this resist process.

5. As you breathe, notice if you feel any resistance to this process. Are you reluctant to let go and be creative? Do you doubt yourself or your efforts? Is there a voice telling you that this is a waste of time, or nothing but foolishness? Stay connected to any thoughts you are having that may be working against you. If you feel nervous or reluctant to let go, simply continue to breathe and draw and let those feelings pass.

6. When you have made a design over the page that pleases you, open up your watercolor set and use your brush to moisten the colors with water. Let the water sink into the paint and soften and liquefy so that it becomes creamy and ready to use.

7. Create a watercolor wash using one of the darker colors, such as black, purple, dark blue, or dark red. In this case, use more paint than water to achieve a full-bodied, rich wash.

8. Paint the wash you just mixed over one area of the oil-pastel drawing and observe the effect of the wash as it flows over the lines. I'm always delighted how the paint jumps off the waxy resist and beads up, exposing the bright colors underneath. What do you feel as you try this process?

9. Paint over the oil pastel with washes of different colors and shapes, and use a variety of brushes. Let your authentic artist self emerge and have fun.

10. When you are finished, take a break and let your painting dry. It shouldn't take too long. To speed up drying, put it in direct sunlight or use a blow dryer.

Using the tools of an artist enables us to draw a strong circle of power. By pressing heavily on our drawing tools, we assert our power, strength, and authentic voice. The more you practice drawing a circle of power at your own feet, the easier it will be to access your authentic voice. Outdated beliefs will fall away, leaving the voice you were born with, your original voice.

Underwater-Scene Resist Painting

Now we will use the resist process to create an underwater garden scene. For this, you will call upon your natural gift of imagination and memory. Everyone has powers of imagination and memory, but some of us don't trust ourselves enough to use these resources. Work from your circle of power and practice relying on your authentic vision.

The Beatles once sang, "I'd like to be under the sea, in an octopus's garden in the shade." In the song, they also mention that there is no Committee in the garden: "No one there to tell us what to do." The lighthearted spirit of this song can inspire us to give in to our imagination and disregard any voices from outside our circle of power.

1. In your mind's eye, bring up some images of underwater things, such as wildly colorful fish, plants, coral, kelp, shipwrecks, pirate's treasure, mermaids, King Neptune, or anything else that comes to mind.

Underwater Scene by Linda Novick (see color insert).

2. Make mental notes of the colors as they come to you: orange sea horses green sea anemones, schools of black-and-yellow-striped fish. Make up any fantastic fish that you can conjure up in your imagination. Keep imagining sea creatures, bubbles, and deep-sea divers. How outrageous can you make this scene? Do you find yourself resisting your imagination? If so, why? Now is the time to rely on your imagination and let it reveal your most gorgeous visions.

3. Use your oil pastels to draw the visions you are seeing. Use lots of different colors, any that seem bright and bold and appropriate for the underwater world you are creating. Remember to press hard so the paper will resist the watercolors later. Give expression to flights of fancy. Go with the flow of lines that "feel" like the sea to you, such as ocean currents, bubbles, waves, whitecaps, schools of fish, tidal pools.

4. When you finish your drawing, paint a wash of watercolors on top of it. Use luscious blue-greens and darker blues. Paint the waves and the ocean currents. Try replicating the effect of the ocean water by using washes of different strengths.

5. When you are finished, let your paper dry. If your painting curls when it dries, place it under some heavy books overnight.

The underwater seascape is unique to you. It shows how painting can help you uncover and build trust in your own way of seeing the world. In fact, no one sees the world any clearer than you do.

You are powerful when you stand in the center of your own circle and trust your own experience of life. You only need to be true to your own urges and motivations to be strong. As Martha Graham said, "There is only one of you in all of time, this expression is unique." It is important to know this and to seek to keep creating using your own special talents and ideas. Take some time to absorb your experience with resist painting. Allow your thoughts and emotions to float in your awareness as you focus on your breath. When you feel ready, you can write in your notebook or your sketch pad any words that come to your mind. If you're not sure what to write, use the questions and phrases below to get you started.

Reflections

What do you believe about artists?

What did you learn about yourself from these resist exercises?

In what ways do you follow your authentic artist's voice?

What do you really love to do?

My circle of power is …

When I follow my authentic vision I feel …

I am afraid to do what I love because …

If I could redraw my circle of power I would …

What I really believe about my artistic urges …

5 STEPPING BACK

CULTIVATING WITNESS CONSCIOUSNESS USING SOFT PASTELS

This body's existence is like a bubble's
may as well accept what happens
events and hopes seldom agree
but who can step back doesn't worry
we blossom and fade like flowers
gather and part like clouds
worldly thoughts I forgot long ago
relaxing all day on a peak.

—SHIH-WU (1272–1352)

Have you ever wished that you could feel less controlled by your emotions and thoughts? By identifying with our thoughts, we are fooled into thinking that *they are* who *we are.* Thoughts and feelings seem so real, we mistakenly believe they are telling us the "truth." Our thoughts and emotions have the power to insert themselves as a barrier to our experience of the fullness of life. The tendency to judge our experience takes much of the joy out of living, because beneath the freshness of the moment lurks the dreaded judgment and the implied question, "How am I doing?"

Painting is a way for us to enter the present moment in a profound way, and to ignore fleeting ideas, or distracting emotions and thoughts. When we can detach from thoughts and emotions and meld into a painting experience we have access into the eternal now. Painting can transport us into a place beyond our ego and help us feel the beauty of each moment.

In this chapter, we'll explore the concept known as witness consciousness, the practice of simply observing our thoughts and feelings without getting caught up in them or judging them. This practice allows your mind to become a witness to its own processes: it can observe its own patterns of thinking, its judgments, its evaluations, and even neuroses. Our body-centered experience will encourage witness consciousness through meditative breathing, and we will have a chance to practice witness consciousness as we play with soft pastels and then use them to draw a still life.

STEPPING BACK WE GAIN PERSPECTIVE

Chinese poet Shih-wu reminds us at the beginning of the chapter that "who can step back doesn't worry." Stepping back can mean getting a better view by standing further away from the situation at hand and taking time to breathe. It can also mean taking our egos out of the equation and becoming more silent by detaching slightly from—but not denying—the events in our lives and our ever-present emotions and thoughts. By detaching and simply witnessing each moment, we are practicing what enlightened masters have been talking about since the first word was uttered.

But how can we do this: step back from being an active participant who is attached to results and outcomes? Is it truly possible to untangle our egos from the events in our lives? I experience this when I am immersed in my painting. My mind doesn't go blank, nor do I go into some kind of trance; it's simpler than that. I just become the observer, and I notice the nuances of my experiences, from the thrill of mixing that yummy turquoise color to the giddy beating of my heart as I apply the paint to the paper.

And sometimes I observe less positive thoughts. Sometimes my mind warns me of "impending doom" and assures me that I am ruining my picture. In the next moment, I have the redeeming thought that I really didn't ruin it, after all. First, a part of my mind hates my painting and then another part loves it! Which part of my mind is telling the truth? When we observe our mercurial thoughts from a place of detachment, we see that they are neither true nor false, right nor wrong. They are just thoughts.

The twentieth-century author, painter, and illustrator Eyvind Earle has alluded to his being witness to the process of creation. He says, "Since I never plan in advance, but rather, simply let myself be led by instinct, taste and intuition. And is in this manner that I find myself creating visions that I have never before imagined. And little by little certain color effects develop that excite me and I find the painting itself leading me on and I become only an instrument of a greater, wiser force … or being … or intelligence than I myself am." By letting his paintings reveal themselves to him, rather than trying to control them, Earle simply observed the process from one moment to the next and let it unfold organically.

Painting is an activity that can bring each of us back into direct experience and the peace of the present moment. It helps us to let go of the past and the future and allows our minds to dwell in the beautiful present moment of creation. Perhaps painters have been so enthralled by this practice because it does bring them fully into the present moment in a compelling way. Working with the painting process is magical and helps artists see things with fresh eyes.

Even though our judging and comparing mind sometimes takes us out of the moment and stifles our creativity, it does not always need to be that way. We can let go of dwelling on the past and worrying about the future and once again find our bliss by fully experiencing now, without judgment. There is a process called witness consciousness that can help us achieve that state of mind.

WITNESS CONSCIOUSNESS

The great Indian sage Krishnamurti coined the term *choiceless awareness* to describe the concept of witness consciousness, a state in which the mind is open, curious, and free of opinions and concepts. This perception of "what is" is sometimes called "choiceless observation" because it allows reality to appear as it exactly and essentially is. It is the ability to comprehend the truth in a flash, the unpremeditated art of *insight* or seeing into what is. Choiceless awareness is allowing the essence of reality to flower fully without the aid of analysis, remembrance, or even understanding from a particular point of view. It is choiceless because you refrain from choosing one thing over another. Choice implies preference, which implies judgment— good, bad, beautiful, ugly. The goal of witness consciousness is to simply observe without using such labels.

I first learned the term *witness consciousness* when I was studying to be a yoga teacher in 1996. My yoga instructors taught me how to witness my experience while practicing yoga postures called *asanas* and learning meditation techniques. When you put your body into yoga postures, you become aware of sensations, which you may label as pain, tightness, or tiredness. The mind not only labels what it experiences, it also evaluates, judges, justifies, and defends. For example, when you stretch in a certain position, your mind may first say to you, "This hurts," and then, "Your body is stiff and inflexible," and finally, "You're getting old and going to pot." If you stop to witness the mind's conversations, you notice how much embellishment your mind adds to a simple moment to-moment experience.

Practicing witness consciousness is particularly helpful when you are learning something new, such as a new painting technique, because it helps you to release your mind into the experience just as it is. It helps you have more fun if you can simply observe your experience, without judging or analyzing it. When you witness yourself painting, your ego recedes into the background. You see the colors flow onto the page, you feel the gooey paint, and simply observe your creation.

In the same way that Degas became the channel through which a greater intelligence communicated, you too can relinquish control of your painting, observe it even as you are creating it, and let it speak to and enchant you. Once you release the idea that you are responsible for making a "good" painting, you can play with it and enjoy all the sensations connected with its creation. You can be more present to your moment-to-moment experience.

APPLYING WITNESS CONSCIOUSNESS DURING PAINTING

Practicing witness consciousness isn't necessarily hard, but it can be challenging because you must continually bring yourself back to the present moment, and your mind naturally wants to think about the past, the future, or perhaps pronounce judgment on the painting you are working on.

The first step is to practice watching the conversations in your mind without judging them. As you engage in the pastel activity at the end of this chapter, try to observe the voices that comment on your experience. For example, after painting a stroke on your paper, if you notice the thought "I made a mistake," or perhaps "I love this!" simply notice the thought and keep going. Don't let discouraging thoughts stop your process, and don't let encouraging thoughts make you take yourself too seriously. Observe the fullness of your experience and be present to it all.

The second step in this process is to keep noticing your breathing. Stay focused on your breath while making your painting. Breathing keeps the flow of life force moving and keeps supplying you with energy. Use the breath as a source of energy and be conscious of the breath flowing into your painting. Breath brings *prana* to your body, and this is transmitted into your painting.

The third step is to drink in all the aspects of your experience, including the sights, sounds, smells, and physical sensations. These will include feeling your heart beating, the warmth on your skin, and the weight of your body. As you move your body, feel the movements your arm is making. Pay attention to the texture of the materials you are using, such as the grittiness or softness of the pastels and the roughness of the sandpaper.

WHY SOFT PASTELS?

Soft pastels are particularly appropriate for practicing witness consciousness because of their evocative, tactile qualities. The author, psychologist, and yoga teacher Stephen Cope said, "Witnessing is a whole-body experience. Instead of an intellectual exercise, the witness receives experience by feeling the reverberations of sensation with the whole physical-emotional organism." Pastels are sensuous and feel good in your hands. They come packed in a box like little colored candies, a delight for the eyes. All your senses will be stimulated by using pastels. When you use them, let your whole body become involved.

The moment you pick one up, you may feel like you know how to use it. Pastel may remind you of the chalk you drew with when you were a child. Or you may be repelled because you fear using them, or cringe at their messiness and how they dirty your hands. These thoughts are OK, too. Stephen Cope also reminds us that "The witness does not censor life … rather allows all thoughts, feelings and sensations to receive the light of awareness without discriminating." It's all right to hate what you did or love what you did, to hate the process or love it. Let yourself simply observe the entire process, being the witness to the whole show.

The term *pastel* does not refer to pale colors; rather the word comes from the French word *pastiche* because the pure powdered pigment is ground into a paste. Soft pastels are made from the same pigments used for oil paints, which have been pulverized and combined with just enough liquid binder, such as gum Arabic, to form sticks of color. They are different from the oil pastels that we have already used in this book. They blend more easily and come in more colors—well over seven hundred colors, ranging from soft and subtle to bright and brilliant. Oil pastels are pretty, but soft pastels are luscious.

Note: Soft pastel paintings require care when handled. They smear, so they need to be stored in a safe place and placed in between sheets of protective paper. Wax paper works well, but the wax can melt in hot environments, such as in a car on a hot summer day. A better solution is to use glassine paper, which is grease resistant, has a high resistance to the passage of air, and is almost impervious to water vapor. The very best protection for a good pastel painting, however, is inside a picture frame. Also note that soft pastels will not resist watercolors, as do oil pastels. They do not blend with oil pastels, nor are they the least bit compatible with them, so be sure to keep them separate.

The versatility of soft pastels has made them a favorite of artists throughout history for a wide variety of projects. Many artists have used pastels for making preliminary sketches because their colors duplicate the colors in an oil painting and can be executed quickly, "on the spot," and later translated into a finished painting in the studio. The Venetian artist Rosalba Carriera used pastels with great dexterity and achieved great fame during the 1700s, painting highly realistic portraits of society men and women. Carriera's ability to convey fine details in hair, clothing, and facial features highlighted the versatility of the pastel medium. She demonstrated her skill as a portrait artist by the careful blending of delicate colors and by capturing the personality and likeness of her sitters. Working on paper, Carriera achieved a highly polished surface that hid individual strokes from the viewer's eye. She pioneered the use of pastels to create finished works of art, rather than simply as a medium to produce preparatory sketches.

DIFFERENT STROKES FOR DIFFERENT FOLKS

There are many different ways to apply pastels, and they are fun to play with on a wide variety of surfaces, from smooth paper to fine sandpaper.

Artists have traditionally used soft pastels on colored surfaces, called toned grounds, rather than white paper. As you explore different colored and textured papers, avoid labeling some as good and others as bad. When we are truly witnessing, we release the temptation to label things or force them into opposing categories such as right and wrong or desirable and undesirable. Labeling tends to shut down possibilities and close off areas for exploration.

While this may be challenging, it opens us up to quantum leaps of awareness and appreciation. The combination of pastels and unique toned grounds enable all kinds of interesting possibilities for creativity. Sometimes an artist will leave parts of the paper uncovered, or just use a few strokes to indicate a background. At other times, the artist will cover the entire page with pastel and create a thick buildup of color.

My favorite surface is the grayish-black sandpaper sold in hardware stores. I recommend a 600-grit surface, which is finely ground and feels like you are stroking a fine suede coat. It is a luscious color too, and every color you apply to it looks good, from subtle earth tones to brilliant high-key colors. When you lay the pastels on their side and stroke them across the page, the sensation is satisfying and sensuous. Because the paper is small, I have produced what I call "little gems," little landscapes, seascapes, and even miniportraits.

Practicing witness consciousness is an ongoing process. As such, it is both easy—you can return to it at any moment, wherever you are, whatever you are doing—and hard, because it is a continual process, not something you achieve once or complete. You simply need to recognize that it exists, and once you do, you can practice and cultivate this enlightened and enlivened state. As you do the body-centered experience and then begin working with pastels, first by practicing various strokes and then by painting a still life, continually remind yourself to return to witness consciousness as a way to become grounded in the present moment and experience the gift of living in the eternal now.

Getting Ready

Prepare your art space before practicing meditation, so you can flow right into the pastel project. You may even want to read through the first few steps of the art project to prepare your paper surface ahead of time. Be sure that you have your pastel supplies nearby so that you can go to them when you're finished meditating.

Let's Connect with
Our Body and Breath

Our yoga-inspired exercise is a simple but effective form of meditation called *anapanasati*, a technique taught by the Buddha in which breathing is used to develop a serene and concentrated mind. By consciously focusing on the minute details of our breath, our mind begins to see into itself and discovers a unique freedom. This form of meditation is said to be the form that brought the Buddha to full awakening.

As you focus your attention on your breathing, you'll be allowing your mind to move as it will, without becoming involved in the thoughts. You will be witnessing your thoughts without paying attention to them, but simply being aware that they are "saying something." You'll simply be the observer, not a participant, in the mind's conversation.

In this process of observing your breath and disregarding your thoughts, you are training yourself to release your identification with your thoughts and even discover who you are behind your thoughts. You become present, watching your breath. Thoughts will come and go, and you'll let them go without attaching to them. This is a powerful way to develop witness consciousness.

In the breathing exercise we practiced in chapter 4 called the three-part breath, or *dirgha pranayama*, you learned to entirely fill your lungs with oxygen. It was a controlled breath in which your intention was to fill the lungs completely and then empty them fully. Your focus was on breathing in a certain way to bring more oxygen to the brain and the bloodstream.

The practice we are doing here is quite different from *dirgha pranayama*. Our practice will be meditation using breath as your focus. You will not be forcing your breath into any prescribed way of breathing by making it slower, faster, or deeper, rather you'll be observing it. At times it may be shallow and other times deeper, but you needn't analyze, evaluate, or control its the qualities.

Note: This meditation is best experienced without referring to the book. Please read through instructions before you begin the practice, or record the instructions and play them back to yourself, making sure to leave enough space between instructions so they will be timed correctly when you play them back.

1. Set a kitchen timer or other alarm for five to ten minutes. (If you find you like this meditation technique and want to continue with it, you can slowly increase the amount of time you practice.)

THE PAINTING PATH

2. Sit on a chair or couch and place your feet firmly on the ground. Let your body relax into the chair. Rest your hands in your lap and let your elbows fall against the side of your body. Consciously relax your shoulders, belly, and any part of your body that feels tense.

3. Lengthen your spine by pressing the very top of your head toward the ceiling. Keep your spine straight but not rigid, as this keeps energy flowing freely throughout your body and prevents sleepiness.

4. When you feel relaxed and centered, close your eyes, or if you prefer, keep your eyes slightly open with a soft gaze toward a spot on the floor. Bring your awareness to your breath, feeling it flow in and out of your body. Let your breath be natural and steady.

5. Notice where you feel your breath the most. If you feel your breath strongly in your chest, then focus on your chest rising and falling, over and over. If you feel your breath in your nostrils, focus there. Notice all the sensations involved in your breathing, such as the temperature of the air as you inhale and exhale. Let yourself become involved in these sensations until your breath becomes your whole world.

6. If your mind wanders, bring your attention back to your breath with compassion and gentleness. It is natural for your attention to be drawn away from the breath, because the mind tends to be restless. Noticing this and gently turning your awareness back to your breath is part of witness consciousness.

7. If you notice yourself thinking, don't cling to the content of the thought. Instead, let the thoughts float by like clouds in a clear sky, drifting away gently. Continue to observe your breath; maintain a straight spine and allow your body to relax even more.

8. Simply stay with your breath. Let the sensations of breathing calm and focus your mind. Watch your breath flow in and out like waves on the shore. Keep your mind on your breath.

When the bell on your timer rings, slowly open your eyes. Gently allow your awareness to return to the room you are in and let go of the meditation. Allow yourself some transition time before beginning the painting project.

LET'S PAINT!

I recommend affixing your sandpaper and pastel paper to a cushioned surface before drawing, because pastels work best when the drawing surface has some give to it. Taping your papers to a piece of foam core works well, as does simply spreading a layer of newspapers on your table as a cushion.

Fixative is often used to "fix" distinct layers of pastel while the work is in progress to give a fresh surface for additional layers of pastel to adhere to. When the artist sprays a layer of fixative on his or her work, the moisture and chemicals in the spray penetrate into the granules of pigment to create a surface that is highly receptive to the application of additional layers of pastel. The fixative actually creates a texture that "grabs" new strokes of color, allowing the artist to build up several colorful layers of pastel. Spraying in between layers allows you to add more pastel and have it stick.

Spraying fixative at the end of a project, however, is discouraged because it does not actually prevent smearing. In fact, the spray can damage the delicate final surface and dull the brilliance of the finished painting. However, if your pastels are very crumbly and you notice pastel dust falling off the surface, it may be necessary to spray at the end to prevent dust from landing on the mat. As you gain experience, you can decide when to fix and when not to fix.

Always spray your fixative, even so-called odorless fixative, outdoors or in a well-ventilated room, as the fumes are not healthy to breathe.

Exploring the Beauty of Soft Pastels

THINGS YOU WILL NEED

- *Variety of objects to arrange in a still-life composition*

- *Box of soft pastels (not oil pastels), at least 36 colors*

- *Vine charcoal*

- *5 or more sheets of sandpaper, 9 by 11 inches, in two types:*

    - *413Q 3M 600 wet or dry sandpaper (grayish-black in color)*

    - *413Q 220 wet or dry sandpaper (grayish-black in color)*

- *2 or 3 sheets of toned pastel paper, assorted colors (at least 11 by 14 inches)*

- *Sheet of foam core or corrugated cardboard, 20 by 26 inches or larger*

- *Roll of masking tape*

- *Newspaper to cover your worktable*

- *Workable fixative*

- *Colorful tablecloth and table*

- *Desk lamp or other source of direct light (optional)*

- *Small box of hard pastels, at least 24 colors (optional)*

- *Tortillon or blending stump (optional)*

- *Colored construction paper (optional)*

- *Larger artist's sandpaper, colored or white (optional)*

- *Latex gloves (optional)*

- *Baby wipes (optional)*

- *Stiff bristle brush (optional)*

Note: Since all paints are made from pigments that may contain toxins, many artists use latex gloves while painting with pastels to avoid prolonged contact with the skin. I especially recommend that students with sensitive skin wear gloves. I do not wear gloves, but I do use baby wipes to frequently remove pigments from my hands.

Pastel Techniques

There are three basic types of strokes we will practice before moving into your pastel still-life project: linear strokes, side strokes, and blending. These three basic techniques will form the basis for your still-life project. See the color insert for samples of these pastel techniques.

As you practice these strokes, remember to periodically take a step back and practice witness consciousness by observing your thoughts. You may notice that you have judgmental thoughts such as "I'm doing this all wrong. I know I can't do this." You may have discouraging thoughts that prevent you from enjoying this practice session. Or you may notice that your thoughts tell you that you are enjoying the process. Or perhaps you will be aware that you are seeing the brilliance of the colors or feeling the texture of the paper. Whatever your thoughts may be, your job is simply to be the observer of your experience, including your thoughts and feelings.

LINEAR STROKES

Linear strokes are used to create lines, as opposed to an area of solid color. The lines can be straight or curved, squiggles or curlicues, flowing lines or short, choppy strokes.

1. Affix a piece of sandpaper and a piece of toned pastel paper to two different cushioned surfaces. It is best to have more than one type of paper on which to practice your strokes.

2. Open your box of pastels and choose a color that you like. Hold the stick loosely between your thumb and index and mid-

dle fingers and touch the tip of the pastel to the paper's surface. Make several short, diagonal strokes on each of the papers. Vary the pressure you use when drawing, and notice the different-size lines you can get with this one diagonal stroke.

3. Notice your feelings and thoughts as you discover how the pastels react differently with each paper. Practice witness consciousness by simply observing your experience, without labeling one better than the other.

4. Choose another color, and make diagonal strokes in the opposite direction, intersecting your original strokes. You have just used a technique called cross-hatching. You can use cross-hatching to blend two colors or to build up the surface of your painting until the individual strokes disappear and all you see is a solid area of color.

5. If you have hard pastels and soft pastels, try using them both to experiment with any kind of linear stroke you can imagine. Play with combining them in interesting cross-hatch patterns. As you experiment, be aware of being the witness to your process, suspending judgment.

6. Try placing short, choppy, slashes of different colors directly next to each other. This technique is called broken color and was used by Impressionist artists such as Degas and Toulouse Lautrec. When viewed from a distance, the individual colors appear to merge into a third color.

SIDE STROKES

Side strokes are beautiful and expressive and are often used to cover large areas of a painting quickly, such as filling in the sky in a landscape or the background in a still life.

1. Take the paper wrapping off your pastel stick. Hold the pastel on its side, between your thumb and index, middle, and ring fingers. Press the side of the pastel lightly against the

paper, allowing the color to glide on and deposit a blanket of color on the page. Use your wrist to twist the pastel in different directions.

2. Depending on the tooth (the roughness or smoothness) of the paper. you will be able to create many different effects using this stroke. If you use less pressure, you will see the tooth of the paper showing through, creating the effect of a textured area of color. If you press hard, you will cover the surface of the paper completely.

Because this technique is so lovely and versatile, you may be tempted to overuse it when you get to the still-life project. Remember that this technique is most effective when used sparingly so that your painting does not become monotonous.

BLENDING

Blending combines two or more colors that are either on top of each other or side by side. This technique works best when you have a thick buildup of color, using side strokes that are next to each other. You can blend with your finger by softly moving your finger across the area that you want to blend. Because fingers can leave oils on the drawing paper, some artists like to use a tortillon, also called a blending stump, instead. This is a tightly wound stick of soft, fibrous paper and is typically sanded to a point like a pencil.

1. Make a linear stroke of red on your paper. Next, make a linear stroke of yellow directly on top of it.

2. Move your finger lightly over the two colors and observe as they blend into a new color, orange.

3. Try blending again using different colors. Experiment with combinations of different strokes: side strokes over side strokes, linear strokes over side strokes, and so on. What effects can you achieve?

Blending can be used when you want to soften the effects of a line or when doing a portrait to soften the eyes or blend the skin tones so the individual strokes do not stand out. Blending is a technique that also should be used in moderation, because too much dulls the surface of the painting and deadens the color. When used sparingly, however, it adds a charming accent to a picture.

Painting a Still Life Using Pastels

Still lifes are a good subject because they can remain in place for the time it takes to complete your work. You can choose objects that may have meaning, such as a special doll or a prized vase or statue. You can practice all the different strokes you have just learned using a still life as your theme.

You will now arrange your own still life that will remain in place until you finish your painting. As you gather objects for your still life, you may be aware of witnessing this activity. What are your thoughts and feelings as you look for the objects you will paint? Simply observe your experience without judging or evaluating it. You may wish to practice beginner's mind while finding objects. If you have never set up a still life, you are indeed a beginner and have the complete experience of doing something entirely new! What is your experience of being a beginner? If you are an experienced artist, what are you feeling now? What are you thinking?

Japan Memories by Laura Riegelhaupt
(see color insert).

Consider using a light source such as a spotlight or a lamp as you did in the chapter on drawing. Placing a light source on the side of the still life will throw the objects into sharp contrast and will emphasize the light and dark areas.

1. Cover a table with a colorful tablecloth.

2. Choose several everyday objects that appeal to you and that are diverse in shape, size, texture, and color. Arrange them on

the tablecloth in a composition that pleases your eye. Use your imagination and play with it until you feel good about the way your objects look. One of my favorite still-life arrangements is an apple on a white plate with a green bottle of Chianti nearby. Another time-honored subject for still-life paintings is simply a vase of colorful flowers.

3. Prepare a piece of paper as you did for the practice strokes, either taping it to a piece of foam core or placing it on top of a layer of newspapers on the table.

4. Gather the rest of your supplies and take a moment to sit still in front of the still life you've created. Witness your thoughts and your feelings as you approach your project. Are you anxious? Excited?

5. Take the vine charcoal, and, using light linear strokes, sketch the outline of the objects of your still life. (Don't use the soft pastels yet.) Look at the outside contour of the objects. Note their placement, their relative sizes, their shapes. Observe carefully, but don't worry about getting the details absolutely correct.

6. After you've sketched in the object or objects, you are ready to begin adding colors with the soft pastels using the strokes that you learned in the previous exercise and any other strokes you feel like using.

7. Start by carefully noting the colors you see in your objects. If you are painting a red apple, what various tones of red do you see in the apple? Are there other colors, perhaps green or yellow, mixed in with the red?

8. Find the colored pastels you will need to paint your still life and remove them from the box. One by one, use them to make strokes on your paper to color in the outlines. Notice your reaction to the feel of the paper and the feel of the pastels in your hand. If at any time you feel nervous or anxious,

return your attention to your breathing, the way you did during meditation.

9. Try to follow the form or the contour of the object you're painting. For example, if your object is round, use rounded linear strokes to mimic the shape as you fill in the color. Where there are shadows, consider using cross-hatching or side strokes. If you want to smooth out an area, use the blending technique.

10. Is there reflected light on any of the objects? For example, a red apple sitting on a yellow satin cloth will create an orange glow on the cloth. The yellow might even be reflected on the surface of the apple. As you notice these lovely tricks of the light, you will be able to see why artists such as Cézanne and French painter Chardin have delighted in painting still lifes over the centuries—there is always more there than at first meets the eye.

11. From time to time, you may find that you have built up layers of pastel so thickly that the paper no long has any tooth to it and additional layers won't adhere. If this happens, take a stiff bristle brush, like an old toothbrush, and brush off the excess pastel and restore some tooth to the paper.

12. Keep working on your still life until you are happy with it or at least satisfied with your attempt. If tension arises, return your attention to your breath and focus on slow, steady breathing. Notice what form the tension takes in your body. What thoughts accompany your tension? Are they critical? You may feel tense because your thoughts tell you that you could have done better. Or you may be appreciative of your efforts. You may even think, "Gee, that looks pretty good." Or you may notice feelings and emotions of peace and relaxation. Oftentimes, being immersed in a painting can have a calming effect on your thoughts and feelings leading to a release of tension. As the witness, all you need to do is watch and observe your experience.

13. When you are done, shake the can of fixative well, hold it twelve to sixteen inches from the surface of your pastel painting, and spray a light layer over the entire surface of the page. (Spray outdoors or in a well-ventilated place.) Later, if you want to, you can continue painting with pastels over the layer of fixative.

Painting still lifes is terrific because it encourages you to look ever deeper into details. Studying a still life helps you to concentrate and be a careful and thoughtful witness to what is—seeing ever more the longer you look.

Witness consciousness is a good practice to employ when you're learning something new, especially painting. When you approach painting with an open mind, you are more likely to enjoy the experience more fully, without the nagging voice of doubt that may appear from time to time. When you notice doubt or fear entering your mind, you can simply witness it and move on.

As you develop your powers of observation without judgment, you may notice your experiences becoming more vivid and infused with life. Whatever you notice, it's OK. Nothing needs to be any different than it is.

Reflections

Take some time to transition into a period of reflection by looking back on your experience of practicing witness consciousness and painting a still life. Reconnect with your breath and allow your thoughts and feelings to wash over you. Begin to notice any predominant thoughts or emotions you are experiencing. It may be helpful to write down some of your thoughts while they are fresh in your mind. Answer any or all of the following questions and phrases in your journal, notebook, or on a separate piece of paper.

What did you notice about yourself while practicing with pastels?

Were you more attracted to or repelled by the pastels?

What challenges did you encounter with the soft pastels?

What did you enjoy most about painting your still life?

How can practicing witness consciousness in your daily life be of value?

The predominant thing I witnessed during this experience was …

I noticed that I have a hard time …

… comes very easily to me.

When I witnessed my thoughts and feelings during this exercise I discovered …

I can see from this experience that …

6

STAYING
FLEXIBLE

PRACTICING IMPROVISATION
WITH LIQUEFYING PASTELS

If you overlook the Way right before
Your eyes,
How will you know the path beneath your feet?
Advancing has nothing to do with near and far
Yet delusion creates obstacles high and wide.

—SHIH-T'OU

The great American violinist and conductor Yehudi Menuhin spoke to all artists when he said, "Improvisation is not the expression of accident but rather of the accumulated yearnings, dreams and wisdom of our very soul." Improvisation is often associated with music, as when a performer breaks away from the printed music, but this is also done in painting, as when the artist stops copying details from a model or sketch and instead paints directly from what he or she sees in his or her mind's eye. This requires flexibility. The artist is not just seeing what is in front of him or her in the moment (as with witness consciousness) but is taking a step forward, even if he or she is unsure where it will lead. In that sense, learning to improvise while painting helps you develop trust in your intuition, which can lead to more freedom, fluidity, and resilience in all areas of life.

In this chapter this frame of mind will be nurtured in two ways. In the body-centered exercise, you will loosen your wrists, shoulders, hips, ankles, and feet using gentle repetitive movements. In the painting project, you will nurture a spirit of flexibility by developing your improvisational skills through a technique inspired by Edgar Degas, in which turpentine is used to transform a pastel drawing into a delightfully vivid and rich painting.

FALLING SHORT OF GREAT EXPECTATIONS

One of the things I love most about painting is that no matter how carefully I plan a project or how meticulously I work on it, the end result is never exactly like I envisioned it. If I sit down in front of a beautiful natural scene, I begin to imagine how I will translate it onto the paper or canvas.

This mental process of preparation and envisioning is an exciting element of the painting process. And it's good to know the direction you're going in— to have a plan for completing your project—but it's equally important not to hold too rigidly to the finished result. Pablo Picasso summed it up nicely when he said, "It's not what I'm looking for, it's what I find."

You may have discovered this in your own art projects: the value of painting lies less in how precisely the finished product resembles your original vision and more in your ability to be continually curious, accepting what shows up on the canvas and pressing forward. The destination is less important than the discoveries you make all along the journey as the painting itself leads you. This quality of flexibility and openness is essential to the enjoyment of your painting experience—and is a wonderful approach to our lives, too.

In fact, we never know how anything will turn out. Spending time obsessing about the future generally only makes us anxious (if we anticipate something bad) or sets us up for disappointment (if our hopes are not realized). Either way, unnecessary mental rehearsals for future events also take us out of the beauty of the present moment, preventing us from seeing what is directly before our eyes. Paradoxically, when we choose to move through life without strict expectations, we find ourselves on the one hand remarkably able to deal with problems easily and effectively and, on the other hand, able to experience real joy at even the simplest pleasures. Being flexible means we can bend without breaking, roll with the punches, and just let things be. We can cope with changing plans without crumbling and meet every circumstance of life with intelligence, intuition, and humor.

In this regard, painting is like a microcosm of our lives. Many of my art students labor to create specific, precise effects that they have envisioned in their mind's eye. Maybe they want to make the bark on the tree look realistic, or try to get waves on a pond to look precisely like they "should look." Invariably, when their results don't match their high (perhaps unrealistic) expectations, they become frustrated, angry, or depressed. In other words, they suffer.

When we try too hard, we disrupt the flow of creativity. On the other hand, when we release the expectation of having a certain result, we are free to embrace the results that we produce and find beauty and loveliness in unexpected places. Fortunately, flexibility in painting, and in all of life's circumstances is something that we can practice and cultivate in our bodies and minds. This spirit of flexibility permits us to explore new territory and know that we will be safe.

THE FEAR AND POWER OF IMPROVISING

One way that we try to control the events in our lives is by writing and rehearsing what we might call "the script of my life." A portion of your script may read something like this: "I'm a terrible dancer. I hate to dance. I embarrassed myself once dancing on a date. I'll never dance again." By telling yourself that you will never dance again, you are attempting to control your experience of being embarrassed.

This strategy may work—you may never be embarrassed on the dance floor again. But this strategy is also limiting, for it could be that deep down you are a terrific dancer but never learned the right moves to gain the confidence you needed. And you never will, as long as you listen to the script and follow its directions. You'll be safe, but you also may be cheating yourself out of a newfound joy.

The scripts we rehearse and follow in our lives are all about control. When we allow ourselves to step outside the confines of the script, we relinquish control and discover we must improvise. This can be scary, because the script, as limiting as it is, also has safe boundaries. Outside those boundaries, anything can go. It's little wonder that we tend to trade the flexibility of uncertainty for the predictability of control.

Luckily, painting is the perfect medium for learning how to step outside the script, outside all kinds of boundaries, all in a very safe environment. Painting can be messy, gooey, drippy, and you never know how something is going to turn out. As you pay attention to your painting as it takes shape, you are encouraged to shift directions unexpectedly, to let the project take a form different than maybe what you had originally intended.

Stepping outside our scripts can also be scary, but the essence of flexibility and improvisation is not to let the fear paralyze you. Artists like Georgia O'Keeffe and Pablo Picasso, who both lived into their nineties, understood this. Yet they possessed the qualities of flexibility and viewed life with fierce independence and courage. Georgia O'Keeffe once said, "I've been absolutely terrified every moment of my life—and I've never let it keep me from doing a single thing I wanted to do." We would be wise to apply this attitude to our process of painting. Despite your fear, paint the next stroke. Trust that your intuition knows what it's doing.

WHY LIQUEFIED PASTELS?

An anonymous painter once said regarding his approach to painting, "If [the figure in the painting] comes out with a blue coat, she must be the Virgin Mary; if it comes out with a beard, it must be Saint Joseph. If I intend to paint a Venus and a splash of green comes out, I know I must paint a frog instead." He nicely captures the unpredictability of art and reminds us that an artist must be willing release rigid concepts and instead be inventive and flexible.

Liquified pastels are particularly suited to encouraging such an approach. This technique was pioneered by Degas, who devised a method of blowing steam onto his dry pastel drawings to create more depth and brilliance in his paintings.

Our technique is slightly different than Degas' method, but the effects are similar. We will start with a soft pastel painting that has the same buttery, velvety smooth quality that you are familiar with from the last chapter, and then apply turpentine to it. The instant you touch your brush filled with turpentine to the paper, the pastels will change consistency and darken significantly. This change contrasts so much with the original application of pastel that it can be quite startling.

Painting over your dry pastel with turpentine is the component that invites flexibility and invention. It also adds an exciting new dimension to your work. When liquefied pastels dry, they darken and form a flat, even surface painting on which to apply more pastels. We sometimes call this flat area of color an underpainting because we then continue drawing on top of this layer of paint. Having a foundation of vivid, saturated colors opens up new opportunities for improvisation through experimenting with new techniques, changing the content of your painting, and trying out new strokes and combinations of colors.

GETTING READY

In preparation for the art project, select a color photograph of a beautiful landscape. You can use a picture from a magazine or wall calendar or, even better, a photograph you took yourself. Choose a picture that inspires you,

a place you can imagine being with the wind in the trees and the sunlight on your face. This will help nurture a flexible and imaginative approach to your painting—rather than woodenly trying to copy every detail from the photograph.

Ideally, the photograph should have a composition of only a few basic shapes—perhaps a wide sky, a pointed mountain, a round lake, and a tall, thin grove of trees—because you will be re-creating these shapes in a more general, simplified way in your painting. See the photograph above for an example of an appropriate landscape for this project.

Next, prepare a piece of sturdy paper for a pastel painting as you did in chapter 5, by taping it to a piece of foam core or by placing a layer of newspapers on the table for a cushion.

Finally, gather the materials for the art project in your studio space so that you move directly into the art project from the body experience. Because this art project involves turpentine, make sure your studio is well ventilated, even if you use odorless turpentine.

Let's Connect with Our Body and Breath

In my painting classes we often practice warm-up movements to loosen and lubricate our joints. My students often report that they feel so much more open to the experience of painting after practicing these movements for a few minutes.

Physical flexibility encourages mental and creative flexibility. The following simple exercises are designed to gently stretch your muscles and increase your body's overall fluidity. They also stimulate the release of synovial fluid, which enhances flexibility in your joints and in turn opens the flow of energy in your body. Stimulating this fluid is like spraying lubricant on a creaky hinge, dissolving rust and enhancing movement. Freeing the body's blockages can also help us release limiting concepts, opening the mind to creativity and inventiveness.

It's OK to refer to the book while you perform the body-centered exercises, or you can read through the instructions several times to familiarize yourself with them. Another option is to make a recording of the instructions, and play them back as you perform the movements.

Note: Do these exercises slowly and deliberately. If you feel any discomfort or pain, take a break or stop altogether. Being flexible also includes the ability to discern what is appropriate for your body.

1. Sit on a chair or a couch with your feet flat on the floor. Lengthen your spine by pressing the top of the head toward the ceiling. Keep your chin in a neutral position, neither raised

nor lowered. Close your eyes and observe your breath flowing in and out of your nostrils, until you feel at ease.

2. Inhale through your nostrils slowly, lift your chin toward the ceiling, and let your head drop back to a comfortable position. When you exhale, drop your chin toward your chest and let it rest there for a second or two. Repeat these movements three or four times or until you feel your neck muscles relaxing.

3. On the next inhalation, lift your shoulders toward your ears and hold for a second. As you exhale, drop your shoulders gently and relax. Repeat lifting and lowering your shoulders three or four times and then rest for a moment.

4. Make little circles with your shoulders by rolling them forward six or seven times. Reverse the direction and roll your shoulders backward six or seven times. Improvise additional movements, such as alternately moving each shoulder separately or anything else that feels good. Remember to stay focused on your breathing.

5. Extend your arms out straight in front of you with your elbows slightly bent. Keeping your arms stationary, circle your hands at the wrists clockwise ten times, and then counterclockwise ten times.

6. Open your fingers wide like a big fan, then curl them tightly into fists. Slowly open and close your fingers, alternating with wide fingers and then fists. Your muscles and joints should be warming up and feeling looser, more flexible.

7. Take off your shoes and socks. Keeping your back straight, lift both legs off the floor. Straighten and lengthen your legs and point your toes. Stretch them as far as you can.

8. Keeping both legs extended in front of you, circle your feet at the ankles in both directions until you feel some warmth

THE PAINTING PATH

in the joints. Alternately flex and point your toes. It is normal to hear some popping sounds as you release tension from your feet.

9. Expand your toes wide like a fan, then close them tightly as if you were making a fist with your toes. Repeat this three or four times. Finally, move your feet and toes in all directions, inventing any movements that feel good for your feet. Place the feet back on the floor and rest. Remember to stay in touch with your breathing.

10. Stand up and plant your feet firmly on the floor, but do not lock your knees. Place your hands on your hips. Make circles with your hips by rotating them to the right ten times, then to left ten times. Start with small circles, then increase the size as you feel your hips began to relax and open up.

11. Improvise any movements with your hips that feel good and visualize your pelvis becoming freer as you do. Releasing the chronic tension most of us hold in our pelvis will make our painting experience a more open and enjoyable one.

12. Finally, raise your arms over your head to form a wide V. Point your fingertips toward the sky, then reach toward the ceiling with first your left hand, then your right hand. Feel the muscles that connect to your ribs begin to open and stretch. This helps open up your waist, chest, and arms and helps your lungs expand to greater capacity.

When you are finished, sit back down on the chair or couch. Close your eyes and tune in to your breathing. Experience the sensations you feel in your body, thoughts. and feelings. Notice any heat, tingling, or flow of energy. Feel how the stretching and breathing has allowed your body to be more flexible, fluid, and relaxed.

When you feel ready to paint, move gently into the art project.

LET'S PAINT!

One way to engage improvisation is to enjoy each step as it presents itself. Try to stay open to the process as it unfolds and release expectations of how it should look when it's finished. Suspend judgment and just look at the strokes you see. Stay curious and open. What colors are nice? What shapes do you find pleasing? Focus on your moment-to-moment experience and be happy while doing it.

Painting a Pastel Landscape

Calm Sea, Maine Rocks by Linda Novick

THINGS YOU WILL NEED

- *Color photograph of a landscape*

- *Box of soft pastels, at least 36 colors*

- *Vine charcoal*

- *Pastel paper of your choice (sandpaper or heavy watercolor paper)*

- *Tracing paper or thin copier paper*

- *Stiff bristle brush (such as a toothbrush) for removing excess pastel*

- *Stiff 1-inch bristle brush for applying turpenoid or turpentine*

- *1 cup turpentine in wide-mouth glass jar or tin can*

- *Roll of paper towels or cotton rags*

- *Hard pastels (optional)*

- *Pastel pencils (optional)*

- *Workable fixative (optional)*

- *Tortillon or blending stump (optional)*

- *Latex gloves (optional)*

- *Baby wipes (optional)*

SIMPLIFYING THE COMPOSITION

Look at the photograph you've chosen and try to find four or five shapes that are most obvious to your eye. For example, the sky might be one shape; the water, another; the trees, another. Simplify the shapes as much as possible. Later, you will add more details.

1. Place a piece of tracing or other thin paper on top of the photograph so that you can see the photograph underneath it. Use a piece of vine charcoal to trace the outlines of the general shapes you have identified in the photograph. Actually tracing the shapes helps you to clearly visualize the composition of the photograph and teaches you to simplify complicated arrangements into their component shapes. Allow yourself to be flexible by not capturing every detail in the photograph—the idea is to keep your composition simple.

2. Hold the tracing of your photograph next to your pastel paper and use it as a guide. Use the vine charcoal to sketch the basic shapes onto the pastel paper with a soft, misty line. Try to keep the same proportions, but stay flexible—you can enlarge the shapes or make them smaller to fit the size of the paper. Feel free to make any changes that you feel like making.

LAYING DOWN THE UNDERPAINTING

When you have a drawing that you like, you are ready to color in the shapes. This will form the underpainting for the project, a ground of beautiful colors that will give the finished painting depth and contrast. See the color insert for an example of how this step should look.

1. Pick one basic color for each major shape you've drawn—green for mountains, for example. Choose light colors for now, because they will darken when you liquefy them. Keep in mind that the colors you choose for your underpainting do not have to be true to your photograph. You could use pink for your underpainting of the sky and work over it with blue pastel later for a striking effect. Use your imagination and intuition. Remain flexible.

2. Hold your soft pastel on its side and apply a velvety blanket of color to your first shape. You can allow the paper to peek through in places, rather than coloring in the shape very heavily. Fill in the whole shape, and don't worry if you color outside the lines. Repeat this process with a new color for every shape.

3. When every shape is colored in, use a stiff bristle brush to paint turpentine onto one shape, blending the pastel into a kind of paint. You'll see it darken immediately. Blot any drips up with a rag or paper towel. On the other hand, you may choose to keep the drips visible as they may lend themselves to improvisation later.

4. Clean your brush in the turpentine, and repeat the process with each shape. When the turpentine becomes dirty, change it to keep your underpainting colors as pure as possible. But don't worry if two edges blend together and form another color. The idea is to create a wonderfully velvety underpainting, and any blending of colors that occurs now can be an opportunity for creativity later.

5. Put the completed underpainting in the direct sunlight to dry, or wave a hair dryer carefully across the page to speed the drying process. If you prefer, leave the underpainting to dry overnight and return to it the next day, when you may have fresh ideas. The important thing is to remain flexible.

PAINTING PATH

***Sunburst* by Anne Katzeff**

Anne played with the oil pastel colors and found she got caught up in the painting, loving the process. As she laid color upon color, the natural curves of the sunburst emerged. She enjoyed the texture of the oil pastels and the way the stick "grabbed" the surface. Working with oil pastels may remind you of coloring—an activity that all kids love.

***Oh, I Didn't Notice That the Canary Was Missing* by Linda Novick**

Inspired by a funny cat I know, I used my imagination and memory to picture it. I began with a pencil sketch and built up successive washes until this crazy cat materialized on the page.

***The Cutest Dog in the World Not Counting Becky* by Linda Novick**

This little dog with spots and a sweet face came to me when I closed my eyes. I began with a pencil sketch to establish the proportions and then added successive washes of color.

Step 1 of the resist process. Use your imagination to draw lines and shapes in a variety of light, bright colors, such as yellow and pink. Draw any shapes that come to you, including squiggles, stars, hearts, or dots. Leave white space on the paper for step 2, adding watercolor washes.

Step 2 of the resist process. Mix bright watercolor washes and paint them over your oil pastel marks. Choose dark colors, such as black, dark green, or purple, to cover light colors. Aim for contrast and enjoy the process. Notice how much the addition of watercolor adds to your drawing!

Underwater Scene **by Linda Novick**
Lively squiggly lines illustrate the dynamic possibilities of the oil pastel medium in this fantastic imagined scene with fish as a motif. Note the tiny beads of paint that appear on top of the oil pastels and the dramatic effects of dark against light. The spontaneity of the resist process invites you to let go of your inhibitions and just play.

**Japan Memories
by Laura Riegelhaupt**
This still life illustrates the power of soft pastels to evoke a mood. Laura lovingly rendered the objects to create a whimsical and sweet picture. You can see the curved linear strokes she used to create texture and perspective on the lamp base and statue. The sparseness of the composition and the use of negative space around the objects heighten the drama of this still life.

Linear strokes

Side strokes

Blending

Notice how lively the practice strokes look on black sandpaper. Traditionally, artists have drawn and painted on toned (non-white) paper, which makes colors stand out and look beautiful.

Step 1: Laying down the underpainting. Using turpentine, blur and darken the original colors you applied to the paper using soft pastels. These bold, simplified shapes invite you to invent and discover while working with the underpainting.

Calm Sea, Maine Rocks by Linda Novick
Step 2: Working over the underpainting. Once the simplified, liquefied underpainting has dried thoroughly, apply soft pastels to create texture, contrast, and lively strokes of color. Working from your original photograph as well as your underpainting, you will invent a colorful landscape from your imagination.

Woman with Umbrella
by Linda Novick

This batik on silk is based on the theme of a Mexican market, where this woman sells her avocados in the heat of the noonday sun, shielded by her umbrella. It demonstrates bold brush strokes created by painting dots, wide strokes, and squiggly lines with hot wax on the fabric. I built up the colors with several layers of waxing and dyeing; the white areas were preserved at the beginning of the process by applying wax to the white fabric.

Painting with wax
After you transfer your simple drawing to the fabric, apply hot wax with a brush to preserve the white areas.

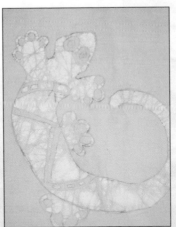

Dyeing the fabric: Day 1
After preserving the white area with wax, dye the fabric and hang it up to dry. See p. 129 for suggested batik color combinations.

Dyeing the fabric: Day 2
Successive dye baths will combine with the color of any unwaxed fabric. Here the original yellow fabric is dipped in red to create orange.

Mummies of Guanajuato, Mexico by Linda Novick
I created this collage by combining different colored and textured papers. The two mummy figures at the left appear to "float" naturally within the abstract composition. Notice the areas of cut and torn paper and the way the mummies seem to fit in that environment.

Self-Portrait
by Laura Riegelhaupt
Laura observed her face while sitting close to a mirror. Lively soft pastel strokes define the waviness of her hair and reflect the highlights of color within her hair. She used bright pastels to bring out the hidden colors that lie just beneath the surface of the skin. Her features reveal intelligence and inquisitiveness.

***Serena, Jack, and Friends* by Linda Novick**

In this oil painting, seemingly unrelated figures occupy the space of the canvas. The figures appear to belong together; they are related by harmonious colors (the result of the color mixing project in chapter 10), repetition of color, and gestures that show them interacting with each other.

Step 1: Arrange images of human figures on Kraft paper. I arranged these colorful figures, harvested from catalogs and magazines, in an imaginative way that creates a surreal scene.

Step 4: Block in basic areas of color with washes. Use more water than paint to achieve transparent washes that allow the canvas to "shine" through. Apply washes within the figures as well as in the negative space; trust your intuition.

A *Brief Bittersweet Autobiography* by Linda Novick

Using photographs from my early childhood and young adulthood, I arranged an evocative and whimsical montage of images. This watercolor painting has a strong pattern of light and dark colors that leads the eye around the page. I used the ideas and techniques of collage, but executed them only with watercolor paint; I created the look of torn edges by painting a thin dark line that suggests a small shadow below each photograph image. Each image has significance to me, but the overall watercolor painting has a universal appeal.

Your autobiography will be unique to you. You may use any painting techniques presented in this book—including drawing, resist, oil or soft pastels, oil paints, watercolors, or collage—or you may combine several methods.

WORKING OVER THE UNDERPAINTING

When the underpainting is completely dry, gather your soft pastels together (and hard pastels, if you wish) to work over the underpainting. You will fill in the details of the landscape now, using a variety of strokes and adding new colors, texture, and depth. You can entirely cover up your underpainting, or you can leave the underlying colors partially visible so that they echo throughout the entire painting. This can create some striking effects. See "Working Over the Underpainting" on the color insert for an example of a finished painting.

1. Take some time to look at your underpainting and see what it suggests to you. What images come to mind? You can use your photograph as a guide, but also allow yourself to remain flexible. Do you want to add details or use colors that aren't in the photograph? This is when you have the chance to improvise the most! Let you imagination lead you.

2. Consider what colors you can use that will harmonize or contrast with the colors of the underpainting. For example, if the sky of the underpainting is dark blue, perhaps applying light blue with side strokes or linear, choppy strokes will have a nice effect. On the other hand, using orange to paint in clouds or a sunset would be striking.

3. Slowly add strokes to your underpainting, adding in details such as clouds, trees, rivers, and whatever else is in your photograph or that you want to include. Watch how the colors flow onto the underpainting. Be patient and flexible and allow the painting to evolve as it wants to. Take the advice of Degas when he said, "A painting requires a little mystery, some vagueness, some fantasy. When you always make your meaning perfectly plain, you end up boring people." **Hint:** If you want your underneath colors to vibrate through the painting, remove the paper from the pastel stick, and hold the soft pastel on its side, stroking lightly and just touching

part of the surface of the paper. This will leave some of the underneath color peeking through. Relax your arm as you sweep the color across the surface, using an open stroke, covering large areas of the page with broad strokes.

4. Let your body and mind remain flexible. Refer to your photograph for inspiration, but avoid slavishly copying it. Degas also reminds us, "It is very good to copy what one sees; it is much better to draw what you can't see any more but is in your memory." Improvisation involves diving into your memory, and resurrecting details and images that have been stored away for years. Let them fly out and onto your page.

As you develop your painting, stop before it gets overworked. Leave something unsaid, unspoken, unpainted. Leave something for the viewer to interpret.

WIPING OUT PARTS OF A PAINTING

However, if you've built up a lot of pastel in one area of your painting and don't like what you've done, you can always wipe it out. When I was a young art student, my teachers often advised me to wipe out an overworked area of my work, and it was one of the most valuable lessons I learned. I still wipe out portions of my paintings because it's easy to work an area so much that it looks stiff and unnatural.

Wiping out a part of a painting is incredibly freeing. You get to start again, instead of clinging to what you've painted. Removing an area in a pastel is the epitome of flexibility—it keeps the painting flowing, loose, and fresh.

1. Stroke the area you want to wipe out with a small stiff bristle brush, such as a toothbrush, to remove the unwanted pastel. Collect the falling pastel dust in a paper towel and throw it away in the garbage. (Don't blow the chalk dust, as you don't want to inadvertently breathe it in.)

2. Spray the area with workable fixative to set it. This will allow you to work easily over the section you just eliminated.

When you are finished, set your painting aside and sit quietly for a while. Return your attention to your breath. What was this experience like for you? Did you find that you wanted to copy from your photograph more than you wanted to improvise details?

I doubt that Degas knew what he was doing when he first steamed his pastel paintings—I suspect he was just staying open, flexible, and making it up as he went along. I am reminded of something else he wrote: "Only when he no longer knows what he is doing does the painter do good things."

Reflections

Take a few minutes to write about your experience in this book or your notebook. Feel free to use the following phrases as a starting point:

When it comes to being flexible in life, I …

When my plans change unexpectedly, I usually feel …

I have discovered that I am more …

I am most happy when I am … because …

I remember the time I had to improvise when …

I am not more flexible in my life because …

7 PURPOSEFUL DIRECTION

PRACTICING BEGINNER'S MIND WITH BATIK

Breath by breath
Choose to stay present
It isn't success you are seeking
But surrender to the flow of energy.
It's not control that matters, but letting go,
Allowing life exactly as it is to touch and change
And breathe through you.

—DANNA FAULDS

When I walked into Jyotirindra Roy's batik school in New York in 1970, I thought I knew a few things about batik, an art form that uses wax and dyes to create paintings on fabric. After all, I'd spent the year before in Mexico learning all about it. My head was swimming with ideas about what I could do with the advanced techniques I was going to learn with Mr. Roy.

Was I in for a surprise! I had no idea what I was about to experience with Mr. Roy, the slender Indian man with the red fingernails. Everything he taught was new to me, including the napthol dyes that used chemical reactions to produce colors rather than the dissolving of pigment in hot water, the method I was familiar with. Because of the magic of these dyes, you could dye two different colors on the cloth at the same time! I also learned to use wax and a brush to create subtle, painterly strokes instead of the flat, simple designlike shapes I had already learned, and how to get a soft, dreamy-eyed quality by painting almond-shaped eyes on lovers, sitar players, and sari-clad women who looked heavenward and made the heart soar.

Working with Mr. Roy had an enchantment of its own. It was fortunate that I quickly learned to set aside everything I thought I knew about batik and simply absorbed what he had to teach me. If I hadn't, I would have wasted my time and energy resisting these new techniques, and I would have missed out on a marvelous experience with this batik master and his magical world of wax and dye. By not clinging to "knowing it all," I could let the whole experience touch me deeply.

Openness is the key to beginner's mind, being empty and open. When we are full of knowledge or even full of ourselves, there's no room to receive the wisdom and gifts of our life's experience. On the other hand, when we are open, we discover a wonderful state of being that allows us to recapture our innate sense of play, wonder, and amazement.

In this chapter, you will dig deeper into beginner's mind and have an opportunity to practice it, first with the body-centered exercise called seagull breath and then with the art project, which is to create your very own batik painting.

WE CRAVE SUCCESS AND FEAR FAILURE

In the poem that opens this chapter, Danna Faulds touches on the issues of success and control—topics that consume many of us on a daily basis. For many of us, by the time we've poured the morning's first cup of coffee, our minds are spinning with the day's plans and activities. What things must I accomplish to succeed at work today? How am I going to get the money for the new car (or clothes or home) I want? Our minds are sometimes so absorbed by these thoughts that we don't even notice when we've finished that cup of coffee. Without even realizing it, perhaps, we have slipped into a pattern of trying to control our day with the goal of achieving success and avoiding failure.

Even the ideas of success and failure are based on a very strict way of seeing the world. How do you even define success and failure? Typically, you have a very clear picture in your mind about what success is, and it's different for everybody. It might be a beautiful house. It might be many children. It might be quick promotions to the top of the company. Or it might even be being a full-time painter! The content of the vision is incidental; what's key is that you have already envisioned a concrete idea of what you think you want and have identified achieving it as success and not achieving it as failure. And who wants to fail?

But what if, instead, as you poured your cup of coffee, you thought, I wonder what adventures today will bring? That might seem silly, and it is certainly easier said than done. But this is what Danna Faulds is suggesting we do, and I think it's a great idea. She uses the phrase "surrender to the flow of energy," which is an excellent description of beginner's mind. She reminds us that even though on one level we do want success and want to avoid failure, that's only because we have already created strict categories in our minds about what that means. What we really want, what our souls truly crave, is to let go of these ideas altogether and cooperate with life as it comes. This is a much more relaxed and sane way of being in the world, I think. As we learn to meet life exactly as it is—with beginner's mind, free from ideas of how things "should" be—we can be profoundly touched by life and let it flow through us, even let it use us as its instrument of creation and expression.

Yet, this might seem like a dream. Somewhere along the line, we may have come to believe that being open to the flow of life could be dangerous—emotionally, if not physically. After all, *surrender* is a strong word and has connotations of failure and shame. Because what if we look foolish? What if we do fail? Just like that, we have mentally circled back around to strict categories of success and failure.

But with beginner's mind, there is no such thing as failure. It's when we accept this, that we find we are open to transformation. Letting go of the fear of failure can open us up to a new world that is infused with energy, vitality, and unimagined possibilities. Even perceived mistakes, aren't. The American cartoonist Scott Adams says, "Creativity is allowing yourself to make mistakes. Art is knowing which ones to keep." I love it! Keeping the mistakes we like can make a really cool batik.

UNCERTAINTY

Beginner's mind can help you transcend notions of success and failure. However, it does ask you to enter into another kind of realm—one of uncertainty. This is another kind of challenge. If you're like me, not knowing what to do next can be quite uncomfortable. Maybe you lost a job unexpectedly. With beginner's mind, you can avoid seeing this as a failure, but the fact remains that you may be in uncharted territory and not know what to do next.

Or perhaps you crossed a landmark birthday and suddenly felt that you had become disoriented in life. The things you thought you would accomplish seem to be receding from your grasp. This can be unsettling, even with beginner's mind! After all, even those of us who claim to be spontaneous still make plans. When was the last time you took a trip without knowing exactly where you would stay and for how many days in each place? We make reservations for everything and often plan things down to the last tiny detail.

French writer André Gide once wrote, "In order to discover new lands, one must consent to lose sight of the shore for a very long time." I love that quote. These words suggest what could be a very scary situation, one that explorers have frequently experienced. "Losing sight of the shore for extended periods of time" leaves us in a long period of "not knowing," and this is hard to tolerate for too long.

A PURPOSEFUL DIRECTION, NOT A DESTINATION

Yet, it doesn't have to be that way. André Gide's image of explorers heading into the great unknown is a perfect image of what beginner's mind really is. You lose sight of land, let go of the familiar knowledge that you have, and enter new waters. And it is certainly true that you don't know where exactly you will end up or what you will discover there. But nevertheless, you have a direction and a purpose.

When I talk about beginner's mind in my classes, some of my students mistake this frame of mind for passivity, or a casual "nothing matters anyway" attitude. Or they might find the uncertainty inherent in the process frightening. But nothing could be further from the truth. Just like explorers have a chosen route and a reason for setting out in the first place—they're not just sailing about randomly—when we have beginner's mind, we still have a purpose and a direction. What we let go of is a certainty that reality will conform to our plans. This is what keeps us flexible and open to all possibilities and allows us to experience each moment fully. If we lose our job, we may not know what is coming, but we still have resources and skills at our disposal. If we have a momentous birthday, we know that we still have dreams we can continue to follow.

Beginner's mind is about being open and receptive, but it doesn't mean that everything that has come before has been erased. In fact, one way in which beginner's mind really allows you to excel is to study a subject at an advanced level; this is what I experienced in Mr. Roy's batik classes. Although I had to empty my mind of preconceptions, I didn't actually lose the skills I had picked up in Mexico.

Instead, I learned to see my skills in a porous way. They were a way of doing batik, but not the only way. In fact, my skills, combined with what I learned from Mr. Roy, helped me to get more creative with my batik. On top of that, beginner's mind helps to keep you curious and eager, which only adds more energy to the whole learning process.

You can practice beginner's mind in everything you do. You could breathe consciously and recapture the mystery and magic of living in the moment as when you were young. When you create your batik, you will take a journey through a world of color, form, invention, and mystery. Batik painting can be a method of recapturing your native creativity and finding a path to what Danna Faulds calls "allowing life exactly as it is to touch and change and breathe through you." How would your life be changed if you lived each day with beginner's mind?

WHY BATIK?

Batik lends itself to the practice of beginner's mind perfectly because it is logical and systematic and yet the results are totally unpredictable. It is the very manifestation of having a purposeful direction, but not a destination. In batik, you apply hot wax with a brush to fabric and then dye the fabric different colors to create a painting. It is a method of resist, similar in principle to the resist projects we did in chapter 4.

Even if you've done batik before, every project is different and brings its own surprises: you never know exactly how the colored dyes will look when the fabric dries. Batik is also playful. You can crack the wax in crazy ways to achieve the crackle that appears when the dye seeps between the cracks in the wax. You can use any images you can think of and any color dyes that you want. You work with the fabric in a collaborative way, and the finished product will reveal itself in time and will have its own special excitement.

The word *batik* comes from an Indonesian word *ambatik*, a cloth with little dots. Anthropologists have found early examples of batik as old as two thousand years throughout the Far East, Middle East, Central Asia, and India. However, it is Indonesia, the island of Java in particular, that is most strongly associated with batik. In the nineteenth century, the art form reached its pinnacle there, and it is still a flourishing industry today. Indonesian batik often portrays mystical and ritualistic characters with flowers, trees, and birds occupying a significant position in the imagery and themes.

You may be familiar with the exquisite Indonesian batik skirts, dresses, sarongs, and large bedspreads that are sold in specialty import stores. These fabrics are often created using a metal utensil called a *tjanting*, which has a little reservoir that distributes hot wax through a tiny spout. It takes great skill to control the flow of wax to create beautiful and complicated designs, which are sketched in before the wax is applied. The *tjanting* can deposit hot wax in curlicues or tiny dots—in fact, in every conceivable pattern. Indonesian craftspeople employ another instrument to distribute wax in intricate patterns called a *tjap,* which is a metal or wooden stamp that resembles intricate filigree. This *tjap* is stamped repeatedly with hot wax to create fabric of great beauty with complex patterns. You will not be using a *tjap* or a *tjanting*, but rather an assortment of different-size brushes to apply the wax. But your fabric can also be used to make pillowcases, clothing, or even lampshades.

Looking at the list of materials and the instructions may be a little intimidating or complicated. While there are more steps in this process than in previous chapters, it is very logical and easy to follow—and amazingly fun! It is not difficult; in fact it has a kind of genius and special charm that is captivating and somewhat magical, especially the moment when you plunge the batik into the dye bath and watch the color spread throughout the cloth.

This process can take a few days to complete, and the finished batik painting is always going to be a surprise, so get ready to be patient and get ready to lose sight of land for a very long time!

Getting Ready

The batik project will take several days to complete. Before you move into the body-centered experience, skim through the directions for making batik and decide how much you want to accomplish in one session, and gather the appropriate supplies nearby.

Note: Batik requires cotton fabric. Wash it thoroughly beforehand to remove the sizing, which prevents the dyes from adhering well.

 ## Let's Connect with Our Body and Breath

This exercise, called seagull breath, uses arm movements that warm and stretch your shoulders, neck, and back. It also expands your lungs in a way that encourages more oxygen to enter your bloodstream. This, in turn, facilitates the flow of energy throughout your nervous system.

Seagull breath is a favorite exercise of my students because it is simple yet very effective. They often tell me that after only a few minutes of this breathing, their minds seem to open to new possibilities and they discover increased creative energy and courage. They also report a significant feeling of expansion in the back and chest area.

Note: Read through the instructions several times until you are familiar enough with them to try the exercise without referring to the book. Alternatively, you can read the instructions into a tape recorder and play them back as you do the practice.

1. Sit comfortably on a couch or chair, or sit cross-legged on the floor In a position that you can hold for **several** minutes. Close your eyes and tune in to your breathing. Notice each in-breath and each out-breath.

2. Place your fingertips lightly on the back of your neck and rest your thumbs at the side of your neck. Your elbows should be pointing out to the side.

3. Inhale slowly and deeply through your nostrils, gently press your elbows back, and lift your chin toward the ceiling.

4. As you exhale, slowly drop your chin toward your chest, round your back forward, and move your elbows together until they touch (or almost touch) each other. On the first exhalation, your elbows should touch at about the level of your chest.

5. Repeat this process several times. Each time you inhale, increase the depth of the breath and feel your chest expanding. As you exhale, round your back forward a little farther than on the previous exhalation. Your elbows will touch each other lower down on your torso on each repetition, but do not force or strain. Listen to your body, and back off if you need to.

6. As you lift your chin and expand your chest, imagine inhaling fresh energy and filling your lungs with oxygen. As you drop

your chin and round your body forward, imagine exhaling tension, carbon dioxide, and other toxins.

7. Repeat these movements from five to ten times, or until you feel energized and your arms and chest have more freedom of movement.

When you are finished practicing seagull breath, place your hands in your lap and relax. Allow your breath to return to normal. When you are ready, prepare to move on to the batik project.

LET'S PAINT!

Note: Because batik uses wax and strong dyes, many items used for creating batik will be rendered unusable for anything except more batik projects. Such items are designated "old" in the lists of materials.

Creating a Batik Fabric Painting

SKETCHING THE DESIGN

THINGS YOU WILL NEED

- *100-percent cotton sheet, white, prewashed, cut to a size you feel comfortable using (size can range from 11 by 14 inches to 20 by 24 inches)*

- *100-percent silk fabric, white, prewashed (optional to use instead of a cotton sheet)*

- *Several sheets of paper for sketching*

- *Brown wrapping paper (sometimes called Kraft paper) or white newsprint, cut to the size of the fabric you will batik*

- *Package of carbon paper*

- *Roll of masking tape*

- *Pencil, 3B or 4B*

- *Ballpoint pen*

Woman with Umbrella by Linda Novick
(see color insert).

The first step is to prepare a small-scale sketch of the design you want to use in your batik. Practice beginner's mind by choosing a subject you've never tried before, or allowing your imagination to go wild. Whatever you choose, you can't fail, because with batik, anything goes.

When I need inspiration or ideas, I sometimes leaf through art books or even coloring books with themes I like (such as exotic animals), as the images in coloring books are simple and well drawn. Have fun and remember that no image is a "wrong" image. Follow the steps below, but let go of fear of failure or of making mistakes. In beginner's mind, there are no mistakes, failures, or ruined pictures!

1. Prepare two or three sketches on paper to explore what design you want to use for your batik. Pictures with only a few basic shapes, such as signs of the zodiac, flowers, animals, or geometric designs often work well, but you can sketch any ideas or shapes that appeal to you.

2. Cut a piece of brown Kraft paper or white newsprint to the exact size of your white fabric. Transfer your image by sketching it proportionately larger on the large piece of paper. When your large sketch resembles your small sketch, darken the larger drawing with a ballpoint pen or a soft pencil such as a 3B or 4B.

3. Place your fabric on a hard surface, such as a firm table, and use masking tape to secure it in place. Place one sheet of carbon paper next to another, carbon side down (touching the

fabric), until you cover the fabric completely. Use masking tape to secure each piece of carbon paper together. Use just enough tape to prevent the paper from moving.

4. Lay your large drawing over the carbon paper. Using the ballpoint pen, trace over your drawing again. Press firmly, because you are transferring the drawing through the carbon paper onto the fabric. If you're not sure it's transferring, lift the paper at one corner and peek at the fabric. If you can see the carbon paper lines clearly, your pressure is correct. If the image is faint, press a little harder.

5. When you have gone over the whole drawing and it is transferred to the fabric, remove the carbon paper and the large sketch. You now have your white fabric with your sketch all ready to be waxed.

Congratulations! You've just finished the first step toward completing a batik. When you're ready, move to the next step.

Painting with Wax

THINGS YOU WILL NEED

• *Piece of cardboard or foam core, cut to the size of the sheet*

• *Old saucepan, about 6 to 8 inches*

• *Hot plate with an adjustable heat control*

• *1 pound paraffin wax*

• *1 pound pure beeswax*

• *Several old artist paintbrushes made of hair, including:*

  • *a 1-inch brush*

  • *Other sizes ranging from number 2 to number 8, depending on the amount of detail in your drawing*

The next step in the batik process is to apply coats of wax that will resist the dye and keep that portion of the fabric white.

1. Look at the drawing you've traced onto the fabric, and think about what shapes you would like to preserve white. For example, if you've drawn an elephant, do you want to keep the elephant white and dye the background? Or dye the elephant and keep the background white? **Hint:** I recommend keeping a large portion of the fabric white, because once an area is dyed, you can't return it to white.

2. Break equal amounts of paraffin wax and beeswax into small chunks and place it in the saucepan. Melt the wax over low heat until it is completely liquefied and begins to steam. Be sure to keep an eye on the wax as it melts so it does not become too hot. You do not have to stir the wax because it blends as it melts. **Note:** Use extreme caution with your pot of wax. Never leave it unattended. Do not allow young children or pets near the wax pot, and place the wire from the hot plate in a secure place where you won't trip on it.

3. Place your fabric on your piece of cardboard or foam core. Dip one of your brushes into the pot of wax and hold it there until the bristles absorb the wax. (Avoid touching the bottom of the pot with the bristles, as they will singe and fall out of the brush.) Then shake off excess wax into the pot, but avoid tapping the pot as you shake the brush. This could spatter wax outside the pot.

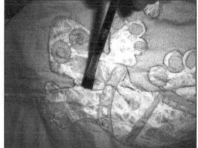

Step 4: Painting with wax (see color insert).

4. Lift the fabric slightly off the cardboard. With your other hand, paint an area of wax onto the cloth. Start waxing in the middle of the shape, and work your way out to the edge of the shape. You'll see the wax spreading out to fill the pores of the cloth. Try to let the wax spread until it comes just up to the carbon paper line, without covering the line.

5. Pay particular attention to keeping the wax on the brush very hot so that it will thoroughly penetrate the fabric from the front to the back, otherwise it will not fully resist the dye. However, do not let the pot get so hot that it boils. Keep it hot, but not steaming too heavily.

6. Continue waxing until all areas of the fabric that you want to preserve white are covered in wax. Turn the fabric over from time to time to see that the wax has penetrated all the way through. If some areas aren't saturated, wax that area on the back side of the fabric.

7. When you think you are finished, hold the fabric up to the light to give you an idea of how it will look when the dye is applied. The areas you waxed will appear light when held up to the light. Picture the *unwaxed* areas of fabric to be the color you want to dye them.

8. If you are finished waxing, unplug the hot plate and let the wax cool and harden.

Dyeing the Fabric: Day 1

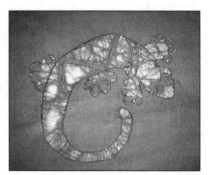

A batik after one dye bath (see color insert).

THINGS YOU WILL NEED

- *Cold-water dyes, including 1 package each of yellow, blue, and red (additional colors such as green, turquoise, and brown are optional)*

- *Large glass jar to dissolve dye*

- *Smaller glass jar to dissolve washing soda*

- *Old spoon for mixing dye*

- *Large plastic basin*

- *Small plastic basin*

- *1 pound table salt (in a box with metal pouring spout)*

- *Box of washing soda (available in the laundry section of most supermarkets)*

• *Heavy-duty rubber gloves*

• *Bar of soap or dishwashing liquid*

The next step is to dye the cloth with a cold-water dye. Begin with a light color, such as yellow. Subsequent dyeings will use progressively darker colors until your final dyeing will be with a dark blue or black.

Note: As you plan your colors, keep in mind that they will combine much as watercolors do, but in often surprising ways. For example, if you use yellow dye first, then blue dye (without applying wax to protect the yellow), they will combine to form green. If you use blue dye again, the green will become even darker. If you then dye with red, the green will become brown. This unpredictability is what makes batik an excellent art project in which to continue practicing beginner's mind. No matter how much batik experience you have, you're sure to encounter some surprises.

You really need beginner's mind with batik, because until you learn how the dyes work on the fabric, you may be surprised at the results. Here's a great combination to try: Begin with light blue, then pink, then yellow, then dark blue. Pink on top of light blue will yield a kind of lavender, then yellow on top will give you a taupe or brownish color. Finally dark blue will darken that color. Leaving it in dark blue for a longer period of time than is prescribed in the dye package directions will give you a very dark blue.

1. Prepare your dyes according to the instructions on the package. The basic procedure I have used successfully is to dissolve one or two heaping tablespoons of dye in a large glass jar of very hot water, stirring frequently with a spoon to dissolve it completely. For larger batiks, use more dye, possibly dissolving the whole package if necessary.

2. Begin with your lightest color, perhaps yellow or a very light blue. You can control the depth of the color by leaving your fabric in the dye bath for a different amount of time than is prescribed on the package. For example, if you want pink, use a red dye, but keep the fabric in the dye solution for a shorter amount of time.

3. Thoroughly wet your waxed batik in the sink or bathtub, using cool or cold water, which will allow the fabric to absorb the dye. Do not use hot water, as it will melt the wax.

4. Prepare a dye bath pouring cold water in the bottom of your large plastic basin. Add approximately one-half cup of salt to the water in the basin, then add the dye mixture and stir with a spoon until everything is completely blended.

5. Wear heavy-duty rubber gloves and plunge your wet, waxed cloth into the dye bath and completely submerge. If the dye bath looks too dark as it enters the fibers of the cloth, you can add a little more water, but remember that the colors will lighten when the batik dries.

6. If you keep the fabric flat in the water, the batik will have a smooth, clean look. If you scrunch it up in the water and allow the dye to go into the rivulets of cracked wax, the batik will have tiny lines of color throughout called "crackle." Using beginner's mind can keep you curious about every part of this process. If you stay open to the dyeing process, it becomes fascinating to watch the dye seep into the cracks and darken the fabric!

7. Stay with your fabric, moving it from time to time so that the dye is evenly distributed in the fibers, keeping it thoroughly submerged. It should rest in the dye bath for about fifteen minutes.

8. Meanwhile, in a separate jar, mix a cup of washing soda with very hot water until it is thoroughly dissolved. Washing soda is pure sodium carbonate, which is an electrolyte that helps set the dye, making it colorfast. Move the batik aside in the basin and pour the washing soda mixture into the dye bath. Thoroughly mix the washing soda with the dye. Let this stand for fifteen more minutes, moving the cloth around occasionally. The dyeing process should take about thirty minutes, longer if you desire a deeper color.

9. Remove the fabric from the dye bath and rinse it in a bath-tub or large sink. Use soap and cool water until the water runs clear. This rinsing removes extra dye that hasn't soaked into the fabric and does not fade the fabric. Avoid letting pieces of chipped wax go down the drain.

10. Hang the wet cloth someplace where it can dry, and place newspapers underneath it to catch drips. Pour the dye-bath mixture down the drain and rinse with water. The cloth will dry lighter than it looked when it was wet.

Reflections

Take some time to reflect on the process that you just experienced. Feel free to write down any thoughts that you have in your sketchpad or a notebook.

> *What was challenging and what was easy?*
>
> *Were you able to experience beginner's mind, without thoughts of failure?*

DYEING THE FABRIC: DAY 2 AND BEYOND

When the fabric is dry, you are ready to continue. Return to the project with beginner's mind by remembering that you have a purposeful direction but not a specific destination.

1. Look at your fabric again. What color would you like to dye it next? What areas or shapes do you want to preserve in the current color? Try to save as much of the light color as you can, because once you dye it the next color, you can never go back to resurrect the lighter color. **Hint:** Remember that the second color you use will combine with the color of your

A batik in its second dye bath (see color insert).

fabric. For example, if your fabric is yellow and you dye it bright red, your resulting color will likely be some shade of orange.

2. Reheat the wax pot on the hot plate until it is liquefied, then use your brush to apply fresh wax to any areas where the existing wax is cracked or broken.

3. Next, apply wax to those areas where you want to preserve your first color. For example, you might have a picture of an elephant that you waxed to preserve white, and dyed the rest of the fabric yellow. As you look at the yellow, you might imagine a sun and a moon above the elephant. Using the same steps as before, you would then wax a sun shape and a moon shape to preserve them yellow and dye the remaining fabric red, which would turn the remaining unwaxed yellow fabric orange. This would leave you with a white elephant, a yellow sun and moon, and the rest of the fabric orange.

4. What could you save of the orange fabric in the next dyeing? You might wax over the orange creating wavy hills behind the elephant and under the sun and moon, or perhaps wax the orange in the shape of a person on top of the elephant and then dye the fabric dark blue. This dark-blue dye would combine with the orange and create a beautiful brown. Because it's impossible to know until you do it, this method of working is a terrific way to experience beginner's mind. After you dye it blue, you just wait and wonder and see what shows up.

5. Repeat the waxing and dyeing process as many times as you wish, remembering to rewax the parts that you've originally waxed. With each successive dyeing process, you will build a symphony of harmonious colors. Save dark blue or black as your final dye to create your darkest colors and accents.

6. Before dipping the cloth in the final dye bath, consider putting the waxed fabric in the freezer for about an hour to chill it. When you remove it, crumple it up with your hands and the wax will crack, creating sharp interconnected lines of crackle. When you dip the cloth in the final dark dye bath, the color will travel throughout the cracks and unify the batik, creating an overall crackle pattern. (Avoid crushing the "frozen batik" too much because it may create too many cracks, which may overtake your batik.)

What happened to the idea of following the sketch that you transferred onto your fabric?

You followed your purposeful direction: How closely did you come to your original vision?

REMOVING THE WAX

THINGS YOU WILL NEED

- *Old iron*

- *Old ironing board*

- *Stack of newspapers*

- *Tongs for dipping fabric in boiling water*

- *Large old canning pot or spaghetti pot*

- *1 cup salt*

- *Large ladle with a long handle*

- *Heavy rubber gloves*

The final step in creating a batik is to remove the wax. This involves three basic steps: chipping with your fingernail, ironing between paper, and boiling in salted water.

1. When the batik is dry, chip off as much wax as you can with your fingernail.

2. When you can't remove any more wax with your fingernail, lay down a layer of newspaper on an old ironing board. Place a thick layer of paper towels on top of the newspaper, and lay your batik on top of them. Next, place another layer of paper towels on top of your batik. You've created a little paper-and-batik sandwich on top of your ironing board. **Hint:** If you cover the ironing board with a very thick layer of paper towels, you may still be able to use it for ironing clothes. However, I recommend using the board for batik purposes only.

3. Use an old iron on a medium heat to iron the paper towels covering your batik, disposing of the paper towels and newspapers as they fill up with wax and replacing them with fresh layers.

4. When ironing no longer removes any wax and the batik appears darker and very stiff, fill a very large pot with water and add at least a cup of salt. The salt is an electrolyte and will help keep the dye in the fabric. Cover the pot and bring it to a rapid boil.

5. Wearing heavy rubber gloves, use tongs to dip the batik up and down in the boiling salted water. Dip quickly, avoiding submerging for too long. Skim rising wax off the top of the water with a long-handled ladle. This process does not influence the colorfastness of the dye. Use extreme caution when skimming the wax! The water will be very hot; move slowly to avoid splashing.

6. Keep dipping until there is no wax left in the cloth. When the fabric once again feels like wet fabric with no residual wax, hang it up to dry.

Feast your eyes on your first batik painting! Beginner's mind is seeing the final result and being surprised, delighted, and amazed. You may like your product very much, or you may think you could do better. Resist judging harshly and simply be open to appreciating the results of the amazing batik process. Beginner's mind also knows that the way it turned out is exactly the way it turned out. Neither good nor bad, just simply your creation!

SOME IDEAS FOR COLOR COMBINATIONS

Below are four suggested color combinations you could try in your batiks:

First Color	Second Color	Third Color	Fourth Color
yellow	bronze (mustard)	fuchsia	dark blue
light turquoise	rose	bright blue	dark blue
yellow	green	red	dark blue
light blue	pinkish red	burgundy	dark blue

Here is another idea that offers you more possibilities. Dip the fabric in two colors at once. Use two small plastic basins or two flat plastic pans, like trays for developing photographs. Mix two different colors and place in two tubs, close together. Place half of the fabric in one pan and half in the other. Avoid dividing it equally down the middle, rather place it diagonally. For example, you may dye red on one side and yellow on the other side. The two colors blend in the middle and form orange.

When the fabric dries, you'll see that it has created several nuances of color, some of which may not even have names. When you wax, save a little of all the colors. Then use two other colors, for your second dye bath, such as turquoise and fuchsia. By dyeing two colors at the same time, on each side of the fabric, you open the possibility of many more colors. This is a place for beginner's mind. Try something really spontaneous and follow your instinct. Keep all possibilities open.

Rumi said in one of his poems, "Sell your cleverness and purchase bewilderment." What was most bewildering to you in this chapter? From time to time we feel challenged and baffled by new things. And then, all of a sudden, it gets easier, and we know what we are doing. And the next thing you know, you know nothing again. I think bewilderment is underrated!

It's useful to return to Suzuki Roshi's words, "In the beginner's mind there are many possibilities; in the expert's mind there are few." The challenge for us is to be a beginner in everything we do. By remaining a beginner, there is the possibility of discovering something really new every day of our lives. Did you ever imagine that you would be creating a batik painting?

Not only is making a batik a great way to explore beginner's mind, but everything in our lives is a potential practice for us. Everything we approach in this way can be a real adventure. If we are willing to not know anything and to be open to experiencing and learning, we will be amazed at what our lives will become.

Reflections

Having been immersed in waxing and dyeing while practicing beginner's mind, it is time to reflect on your experience. Use beginner's mind to answer the following questions and complete the following phrases. Write in a notebook or journal and be open to anything that shows up, as there are many possibilities.

> *How do you feel being a beginner?*
>
> *Would you rather be an expert or a beginner?*
>
> *Do you always have to know how things will turn out?*
>
> *What surprised you most about batik?*
>
> *How did the breathing exercise affect your painting experience?*
>
> *What emotions did you experience during practicing batik?*
>
> *When I let go of control and go with the flow …*
>
> *Being a beginner makes me feel …*

Being empty and open can lead to …

Success means …

Failure means …

If I truly allowed myself to be a beginner, I think …

UNCOVERING YOUR DREAMS

DISCOVERING THE POWER OF IMAGES THROUGH COLLAGE

There is vitality, a life force, energy, a quickening, that is translated through you into action and because there is only one of you in all of time, this expression is unique. If you block it, it will never exist through any other medium and be lost. The world will not have it. It is not your business to determine how good it is nor how valuable nor how it compares with other expressions. It is your business to keep it yours, clearly and directly, and to keep the channel open. You do not even have to believe in yourself or your work. You have to keep open and aware directly to the urges that motivate you. Keep the channel open.

—MARTHA GRAHAM

One summer I taught a painting workshop in the Italian town of Assisi. One evening as I wandered through and explored the cobblestone streets, I began stopping by little shops and vendors and purchasing papers with Italian designs and pictures of saints, as well as old maps and stamps. I wasn't sure why I was buying these things—they just seemed to call to me.

Later, when I got back to my hotel room, I began assembling these scraps of paper on my desk, trying out various configurations. I hadn't planned on doing this, either, but something just felt right about it. Before long, I realized that I was creating a collage! What I discovered emerging in my soul as I played with those items, moving them about, was the profound respect I had been gaining for St. Francis, the gentle soul and patron saint of animals, who lived in Assisi. I hadn't thought too much about him in a conscious way during my painting seminar, but clearly something in the back of my mind had been paying attention and now wanted to find expression.

So I decided to follow my intuition. I went to a nearby store and purchased some gold paint, along with a few other colors and supplies. I returned to my collage, adding layers of gold paint in between the images and even painted on top of the maps and stamps creating multiple levels of textures and colors to resemble the ancient Italian walls. Finally, I made a glaze of a brownish gold color and painted it over the collage, giving the images the feeling of age and wear. The last thing I did was to paint a varnish over the collage, sealing the images and making them sparkle like gems you might find buried in an ancient vault.

What I discovered from my collage was the deep attraction to St. Francis that I felt, even though we were separated by centuries. What I had been learning about him—his devotion, his gentleness, his commitment to his calling—had sparked within me a deep desire to remember and follow my own calling. Because my subconscious had free reign to tear and rip papers and assemble them in any creative and fun way I wanted to, collage helped give that desire expression.

I believe that we all have deep and unexpressed beliefs, feelings, and dreams that we may not be aware of consciously, but that nevertheless drive and motivate us. In this chapter we will begin to uncover these through yogic breathing and by creating a collage.

WHAT DO YOU WANT?

Children know exactly what they want and usually don't have much difficulty expressing their desires in clear, concrete terms. Ice cream. A doll. A bicycle. Whatever it is, they identify it and do what they can to get it. And if they are refused, they might scream about it! Children have not learned to suppress their wishes.

As adults, we don't always have the same clear access to what we want. It may be that when we were younger, we did not get something we had hoped for and decided we'd never get it and so we stopped looking. Or maybe we became convinced that what we wanted was frivolous, impractical, and we had better set our sights on other things. My students tell me that one all the time. They wanted to paint, maybe even be a professional artist, but for any of a number of reasons, they set aside that dream and pursued other vocations and hobbies.

And yet our dreams—the things we truly want for ourselves in our soul, in that field beyond right and wrong—never really go away. They linger, often just below the surface of our everyday conscious mind. They percolate away with an energy all their own, just waiting for an opportunity to be identified and expressed.

So how do you uncover what you really want? Images can be a remarkably powerful tool for that. Have you ever browsed through a catalog or magazine and something caught your eye and unexpectedly thrilled your soul? I have a friend who told me he ran across an image of a man in a sailboat on the high seas, crossing the ocean all on his own, destination unknown. As a boy, my friend had spent time on similar sailboats and had dreamed one day of sailing around the world. He had long ago abandoned that dream, but when he saw that picture, the old desire came rolling back with power and poignancy. It had never really gone away.

NO, WHAT DO YOU REALLY WANT?

In the quote that begins this chapter, Martha Graham says that we each have a vitality or life force, that is unique to us. Our job, she says, is to keep the channel to that vitality open so it can find expression in the world.

I think this vitality is tied to the things we want. It's a kind of motivation, a drive that leads us, often subconsciously, to do the things we do. And it may be that it's this deeper motivation—instead of the object of our desire itself—that is the really crucial part of expressing what we really want.

For example, my friend's dream to sail around the world by himself may not be a realistic goal for him any longer. But by uncovering and reflecting on that dream, he may discover the deeper motivation behind it, that is, that ever since he was a child, he yearned for independence and freedom. Understanding this deep energy, in turn, might help him understand some of the career and relationship choices he has made in his life and lead to greater self-understanding. It might also spark ideas for other hobbies or activities he can do to honor and nourish his desire for independence if sailing around the world doesn't work out.

WHY COLLAGE?

The collage artist rarely begins with a preconceived idea of a finished product. Instead, the collage evolves from the process of finding, assembling, and then pasting images onto a surface. Whereas the painter often decides what he or she wants to paint, finds a model or a still life, and then paints what is before him or her, the collage artist often starts with only a vague idea and slowly builds the collage up, finding images from a wide variety of sources and assembling them until the collage is complete.

The stuff of collage may include photographs, old postage stamps, and assorted papers, often juxtaposing unrelated or incongruent elements to form a mélange of images. Collages are powerful because of the impact of seeing these evocative images.

Making collages allows you to experiment with images (which can include words, letters, or actual objects) that can transcend the everyday logical functioning of your mind and give life to you visions and aspirations that may have been hidden from your conscious minds. Collage is especially suited to this because it uses imagery, rather than a concrete object, a still life or landscape, that is reproduced. We follow our urges, rather than formulas and strategies that come from the past.

You can approach collage with beginner's mind, letting yourself be carried away by your momentary urges, the way children are. Perhaps that's why children love to cut and paste, because there is no right or wrong when doing this. Collage offers the artist flexibility and free range of the imagination. I still love the process of making a collage—of cutting, tearing, ripping, and pasting, almost willy-nilly at times. It allows me to respond to my own internal, hidden motivations and messages, rather than the messages and concepts the world sends my way. And besides that, it's fun!

COLLAGE: IT'S NOT JUST FOR KIDS ANYMORE

Occasionally, some of my students balk at the idea of creating a collage. They have memories of making collages in grade school, and they have lingering beliefs that collage is nothing more than a rainy-day activity for schoolchildren.

Nothing could be further from the truth. Collage is, in fact, a profound art form that has a respected history among some of the twentieth century's most revered artists. Robert Motherwell, the American abstract painter, even claimed that "collage is the twentieth century's greatest innovation."

Whether this is true is open to discussion because there are examples of creations made of cut, torn, and pasted paper before the twentieth century. In fact, the history of collage goes back to the invention of paper in China in about 2000 BCE. We see examples of collage in all civilizations throughout history and in every culture. Native and indigenous societies throughout the world used beads, shells, feathers, and butterfly wings to enhance masks, pottery, baskets, and clothing, both for decoration and as symbols of spiritual and religious power. More recently, the Victorian era was enamored of valentine greeting cards adorned with hearts and lace.

But Motherwell is right in that collage really came into its own in the 1920s among artists such as the Spanish painter Picasso, the French artist Braque, and the German artist Schwitters, who pioneered new techniques and plumbed the depths of collage. Braque and Picasso worked together creating the movement known as Cubism, in which the painter looked at objects from multiple viewpoints all at the same time, and they simultaneously developed the collage. While Picasso's *Still Life with Chair Caning*, completed in May 1912, is often considered the first modern collage, it is actually an assemblage of oil paint, oilcloth, pasted paper, and rope, making it a low-relief, three-dimensional construction. This highly inventive creation set the precedent for future collages, opening the door for artists to use a vast array of materials.

Perhaps most striking were the collages created by the Dadaists. Begun in the 1920s in Germany, Dadaism shattered the rules that up until this time artists had followed, opening the door to unlimited artistic expression. In German, *dada* is a nonsense word, meaning "nothing at all." Shocked and sickened by the amputations of soldiers returning from the battlefields of World War I, the Dadaists created collages by cutting up pictures and assembling them in shocking ways. They created frightening images of soldiers with false noses, limbs, and other body parts. They blurred the boundaries between art and society by incorporating parts of machinery, newspaper clippings, and food labels in their collages, partly to show the public that art was not only for an elite group of artists but could be accessible to anyone.

Salvador Dali, another noted painter, said, "Surrealism is destructive, but it destroys only what it considers to be shackles limiting our vision." The Surrealist movement grew out of Dadaism and developed in response to the new emerging science of psychology introduced by Sigmund Freud. The Surrealist artists and writers of the 1940s were inspired by the world of dreams and the unconscious mind. As a result, they created paintings and collages that juxtaposed and combined seemingly incongruent objects and placed them in puzzling situations. The resulting artwork was shocking, frightening, humorous, and often enigmatic and helped uncover the power of the subconscious mind.

You can tap into that same dream-uncovering power in your own collage. Uncovering images and dreams from your imagination will open you up to untold creativity.

The great French painter Henri Matisse late in his career began experimenting with paper cutouts, which he made into collages. His assistants painted white paper with gouache paint (opaque watercolor) to give it a bright color. Then he cut out shapes, arranged them, pinned them into

137

place, and finally glued them down on a sheet of paper. He cut the shapes himself and called it "drawing with scissors." He said that the weight of the paper against the scissors reminded him of making sculpture. This technique forms the basis for this chapter's collage project.

Getting Ready

Collage making is an art form that can be done with few steps in an afternoon, or it can be an elaborate project created over several days or even weeks. Before you begin the body-centered exercise, skim the directions for making a collage and decide how much you want to do in one session, then gather the supplies you will need in your studio space so you can transition easily from the breathing exercise into the art project.

Let's Connect with Our Body and Breath

Our body experience in this chapter is a breathing technique called alternate nostril breathing, or *nadhi shodhana* in Sanskrit. *Nadi* means "channel" and refers to the energy pathways through which *prana*, the life-force energy in the body, flows. *Shodhana* means to cleanse or purify. Hence, *nadi shodhana* purifies through breathing the pathways of our *prana*, our life force.

Unlike some of the other breathing practices we have done that energize the body and mind, this technique is used to balance the hemispheres of the brain to foster a state of calm equilibrium and receptivity. In such a balanced state, we are more able to uncover and give expression to the hidden thoughts and dreams that lie just below our everyday consciousness.

Note: Read these instructions several times until you are familiar enough with them to practice without referring to the book. If you prefer, you can read the instructions into a tape recorder and play them back as you practice. Blow your nose gently before practicing to allow your breath to flow more smoothly.

1. Sit comfortably on a chair or couch, and let your hands rest lightly in your lap. Gently bring your attention to your breathing, without trying to alter your breath.

2. Close your eyes and observe the natural flow of your breath. Lengthen your spine by pressing the top of your head toward the ceiling. Let any thoughts that enter your mind float in and out of your consciousness like clouds passing on a sunny day.

3. Lift your right hand and fold your middle finger and index finger down, tucking them into your palm. Leave your thumb, ring finger, and pinky open.

4. Use your right thumb to close your right nostril. Exhale, and then inhale through your left nostril.

5. Release your right nostril and close your left nostril with your ring finger. Exhale, and then inhale through your right nostril.

6. Alternate breathing between your two nostrils in this manner. Establish a slow and steady rhythm. Keep your breath soft and smooth.

7. Focus on your breath and let all thoughts float out of your mind. Become aware of a sense of slowing down and turning inward. If you want to intensify your focus, bring your awareness to your "third eye," a place just between your eyebrows that is inside your head, roughly one inch behind your forehead. As you gaze within at this spot, sense the darkness and quietness of this spot, known as *ajna chakra,* which corresponds to the pituitary gland. This third eye is known as a place of wisdom, enlightenment, and intuition in both Eastern and Western religions.

Uncovering Your Dreams

8. Perform this for four or five minutes, or until you feel relaxed. When you are ready, exhale a final time through the right nostril to end your *nadhi shodhana* practice.

When you are finished, return both hands to your lap and slowly open your eyes. Allow your breath to return to normal and take some time to sit and just observe how you feel. Take a few minutes before moving on to your collage project.

LET'S CREATE!

Very often our dreams and aspirations lie buried just beneath the surface of our everyday consciousness. By using found or created images in intuitive but unexpected ways, you can begin to uncover those dreams in a gentle and inviting way.

Exploring Collage: Finding Expression through Cutting, Pasting, and Painting

Mummies of Guanajuato, Mexico by Linda Novick (see color insert).

THINGS YOU WILL NEED

- *Watercolor set*
- *Watercolor paper*
- *Oil pastels (optional)*
- *1 pint white tempera paint*
- *White glue or découpage medium (also known as matte medium or gel)*
- *Small stiff bristle brush to apply glue or matte medium*
- *White plastic palette for mixing colors*

- *Boards to mount your collage, such as foam core, oak tag, cardboard, cardstock, or other heavyweight paper*

- *Sharp scissors (small ones work better)*

- *Variety of materials with personal significance to arrange and paste on your collage. Use your imagination and intuition to select any items that you want. Here are a few suggestions:*

  - *Photocopies of vintage photographs (save the originals)*

  - *Sheet music*

  - *Cigar labels, matchbooks, vintage wine labels*

  - *Old maps, postcards, letters, canceled stamps*

  - *Scraps of wallpaper or fabric*

  - *Rubber stamps, colored inks*

  - *Tempera paint, colored pencils*

  - *Beads, glitter, buttons, feathers*

  - *Special papers (rice paper, handmade paper, decorative gift-wrapping paper, marbled paper)*

PAINTING YOUR OWN COLLAGE PAPERS

The first step is to paint several watercolor papers for your collage. This is a chance to really let loose with your imagination and your watercolors, because later you will tear and cut them into pieces to glue onto your collage. You will use a few different techniques to make your own papers, such as blending, resist, and making patterns.

1. Paint a few sheets by experimenting with color blending. Try mixing your watercolors in combinations you haven't tried before, and try adding white tempera paint, which will lighten the value of the colors and add body to the paints. Create whole sheets with just one color and others with many

colors. Let your intuition guide you. Keep breathing and stay in the moment with your experience. When each sheet is finished, put it aside to dry.

2. Paint a few sheets with patterns such as polka dots, stripes, or herringbone. Are there any images percolating up from your subconscious? If so, paint the image repeatedly on the paper to create a pattern. Let your ideas flow. Put each sheet aside to dry.

3. Paint a few sheets using the resist method. Use oil pastels to cover the whole page with shapes, patterns or images that compel you. When you are finished, paint over them with multicolored watercolor washes. If you're ambitious, plunge your waxed paper into a dye bath, like batik. Set these papers aside to dry.

Feel free to prepare additional papers with the other painting techniques we have explored in this book, including pastels, pen-and-ink washes, pencil, charcoal images, or batik. The beauty of collages is that anything goes!

CUTTING AND TEARING SHAPES FOR YOUR COLLAGE

The next step is to cut and tear the papers you have painted into shapes to paste onto the collage.

1. Lay out the painted sheets you have prepared. Choose the paper that you like the most and use scissors to cut out shapes. Do it freehand, making it up as you go along, or cut out specific shapes like dogs or trees. Don't worry about proportions or getting it to look exactly like the object. The idea is to let it flow and keep the channel open. Try round amorphous shapes, or angular geometric shapes.

2. Experiment with tearing tiny pieces to use like mosaics, or tear large shapes. Tear skinny shapes and jagged shapes. How

does it feel to cut and tear the papers you created? Keep the channel open to whatever feelings arise.

ASSEMBLING THE COLLAGE

Next, arrange the cut and torn papers on your backing board to create the collage itself. Let your intuition be your guide regarding what papers to use and what composition they will take.

1. Lay out the paper shapes you have cut and torn. Are any of them particularly interesting? Separate your favorites from the least favorites.

2. Place your backing board on a table and arrange your paper shapes in a way that pleases you. Move the shapes around to see what different effects you can create.

3. When you have a composition that lights you up, use a stiff bristle brush to apply white glue to the back of each piece of paper and glue it to the board. **Note:** An alternative to white glue is matte gel medium. Apply it to your papers like glue, and then brush a thin layer on top of the paper. This will make the paper lie really flat and also protect the surface of the collage.

ADDING TO YOUR COLLAGE

If you are pleased with your collage, you can stop right there. On the other hand, you might find that there is a theme emerging in your collage. Perhaps the shapes in the collage resemble musical notes, and you're beginning to recall how you wanted to be a rock star when you were younger. Whatever the theme, if you want to explore it further, add pictures, objects, and otherwise build up your collage. Consider these techniques:

- Look through colorful sports, nature, fashion, and architecture magazines. Cut or tear out any images that you like for any reason whatsoever, and paste them onto your collage. Don't limit yourself to photographs—cut words or even individual letters that will contribute to the meaning of your collage.

- Browse through your old photo albums to find pictures that match your theme. Make photocopies to use in the collage.

- Look through your personal mementos to see if anything sparks an idea. Anything goes—vintage wine labels, old concert tickets, even dried petals from a flower you received from a special someone. If you can paste it onto the collage, why not do so?

- What about other objects that would add symbolically to your collage's theme, such as buttons, old pieces of cloth, medals, medallions, or little toys? Remember that you can write on your collage, also, maybe using a fat marker or a glitter pen. With collage, if you can dream it, you can do it.

- You can make your collage three-dimensional by gluing a small box, such as a matchbox, upside down on the surface and then attaching images to the bottom of the box. Using the center of a roll of paper towels or toilet paper can add another three-dimensional element to your collage.

The Surrealists showed us that our interior life, including dreams, hopes, and unconscious desires, have a way of surfacing in art through symbols and meaningful images where they can be examined in the light of consciousness. What deeper motivation are you expressing through your collage? Remember, your collage does not have to make sense in any conventional way. As you continue to build your collage, trust your urges and intuition. Keep the channels open and allow your dreams to be expressed.

Reflections

Take a moment to write in this book or a notebook. Use the questions and phrases below to help you get started:

What did you learn from your collage-making experience?

What has been hidden from view that you uncovered?

What dreams have you put away because you think they are unattainable?

If you could do it, what would you do?

Now I know I can keep the channel open if I ...

My hopes and dreams are ...

My creative urges ...

BUT DOES IT LOOK LIKE ME?

PRACTICING NONJUDGMENT WITH SELF-PORTRAIT

If you want to be free,
Get to know your real self.
It has no form, no appearance,
No root, no basis, no abode,
But is lively and buoyant.

—LINJI

One of the most revered and expressive forms of painting is the self-portrait. At first, this might seem contrary to reason. After all, self-portraits are just pictures of faces, right? To be sure, when we paint self-portraits, we are painting likenesses of ourselves, including our physical traits. But if you've painted a self-portrait before, you know how much more expressive it can be than simply recording what you look like. A self-portrait can express anything you think, feel, and believe about yourself, society, life, even God. Because you are painting the topic you know best of all, yourself, you can capture every nuance and subtlety that you want to.

The Mexican painter Frida Kahlo echoed this sentiment when she said, "I paint self-portraits because ... I am the person I know best." Her words are true: you are the one who looks at yourself in the mirror every day. But this intimate knowledge of your face and of your*self* can also lead you into (usually negative) judgments about everything about yourself—the way you look, the way you *are*.

Yet, painting yourself can help you to experience yourself in a totally new way, and it can also be an opportunity to behold yourself without judgment. In fact, it can be an opportunity to cultivate compassion for yourself. In this chapter, you will practice this first by giving yourself a gentle face massage to help you know yourself more intimately, and second by painting a self-portrait using pastels, learning to look at yourself with curiosity and fascination, open to what you discover as you gaze into the mirror.

LOOKING IN THE MIRROR

How many times in your life have you walked by a mirror and glanced fleetingly at your image, either admiring or disliking what you see? When we are young children, we quickly learn what the preferred physical characteristics are, and we decide whether or not we possess them. There are many mirrors through which to view, judge, and evaluate ourselves. We even use photographs as a kind of mirror to view ourselves and judge and evaluate ourselves through the information we receive from them. The first "mirror" that I remember looking into was a photograph taken when I was about seven years old.

Miss Anna's School of Dance had a recital, and photographs were taken of all the dancers in their costumes. I was paired with an unusually skinny girl whose bones supported barely visible muscles and virtually no body fat. We were posed next to each other, wearing our pink satin costumes and toe shoes, mirroring each other's movements—one leg extended with toes pointed, arms curved gracefully at the waist, gently bent at the elbow. When I saw the photograph and gazed at my muscular legs and substantial thighs and calves, I knew in an instant that something was very wrong with my body. It was much too big! I knew it! I was struck with a perceived "truth" that was to haunt me throughout my life.

A very wise yogi named Swami Kripalu once said, "Self-observation without judgment is the highest spiritual practice." By that, of course, he was inviting us to make note of our perceived faults without condemning them or beating ourselves up over them. But he meant more than that. He continued, "It is not proper to say that by self-observation you see only your faults. Only when you have the ability to see your high qualities do you have self-observation." What a wonderful idea! Seeing without judgment also means that we can clearly see our strengths and beauty, too. This "highest spiritual practice" is seeing all of us, every aspect, and accepting ourselves for who we are.

Nevertheless, in our day-to-day lives, we tend to make judgments about ourselves when we look in the mirror, ranging from the size of body parts to height, weight, and color of hair, eyes, and skin. We also judge our mental capacities, character flaws, and talent or lack of it. For example, you may tell yourself that you're smart, but have absolutely no artistic talent, or that you're a good person but wish you weren't so messy or could learn to manage money. The string of judgments goes on and on. This harsh and judging mind can lead to constant unhappiness and prevent us from growing and reaching our full potential.

The spiritual teacher and psychotherapist Dick Olney said, "Self-criticism or self-judgment is self-hatred. It will always hurt you. There is no exception to that." This statement may sound strong, but it contains a great truth. As I understand it, when we judge ourselves, there is no love in that process, rather criticism, which makes us unhappy.

Swami Kripalu said, "Each time you judge yourself, you break your own heart." This is the element of self-judgment that is so damaging.

ACCEPTING YOURSELF AS YOU ARE AND ARE NOT

Self-observation is not a complicated process and needn't involve judgment. The judge is the voice within us that is vigilant; this voice will search to find fault and blame. Our inner judge tells us what we did wrong and also constantly reminds us of our shortcomings. Our judging mind evaluates and analyzes our behavior. In chapter 4, we called this the Committee, a name that my friend Debra called her collection of judgmental voices.

Observation is not judging. Rather that process simply watches, noticing everything—how we think and feel, including our fears, judgments, neuroses, or our habitual thoughts. We can learn to look at ourselves objectively, noticing our strengths and weaknesses. These so-called strengths and weaknesses are merely judgments too. So instead of labeling and evaluating, we might choose to simply observe our behavior and thoughts. Nothing more is required.

In chapter 5, we investigated the spiritual theme known as witness consciousness. We found that in this state of being a witness to our thoughts and feelings, we could "step back" and look at everything with more objectivity. In fact, by stepping back we get a much different perspective. We are no longer hopelessly entwined in our thoughts and feelings; rather, we are merely observing them. Now we can take witness consciousness one step further and turn it on our whole selves—observing dispassionately and without judgment not just our thoughts and feelings but also everything else: what we look like, what we have done or failed to do, even what we believe.

SELF-OBSERVATION WITHOUT JUDGMENT LEADS TO COMPASSION

A remarkable thing happens when we look at our whole selves without judgment: we discover compassion for ourselves.

Just how does self-observation without judgment lead to compassion for yourself? It can be different for each one of us. For me, I think it has to do with self-acceptance; noting all parts of myself and letting them all be as they are. It's being able to accept the side of me that panics when I lose my keys or even the part of me that is disdainful of others or intolerant of boring people. It is the ability to recognize my brilliance, funniness, and true zaniness. It's being able to celebrate the really cool things about myself. For me, it's about forgiving myself for the unkind things I've done and congratulating myself for how I stick to things. What is amazing is that I am generous and selfish, gregarious and introspective. The more of myself that I accept, the more compassion I have for myself.

Carl Jung said, "The most terrifying thing is to accept oneself completely." I wonder why many of us have such a hard time accepting ourselves. Once we do accept ourselves fully, it opens the door to so much more ease.

It has been said that once we develop compassion for ourselves, it naturally flows to other people. Being able to accept ourselves for all our qualities enables us to grant that to others. If we haven't accepted ourselves, it can be hard to tolerate others. Having compassion for ourselves, in turn, helps us look on others with nonjudgment and have compassion for them.

WHY SELF-PORTRAIT?

Painting your self-portrait while observing yourself through the eyes of compassion and nonjudgment can be a wonderful experience. You will not only see your physical appearance, but also a deeper reality, by glimpsing your heart and soul. Painting your own portrait will allow you to gaze into your own eyes. You will have a chance to observe your features.

You may see yourself for the first time, clearly, without judgment. You will get to look at your features, your hair, your neck, shoulders. You'll be able to enjoy the colors in your skin, and besides observing yourself, you can be the witness to the whole experience. During this project, you'll get a chance to be with yourself in an intimate way.

As you work on your portrait, you may have thoughts, memories, longings, and feelings of joy and peace. You meet yourself in the mirror and get to be with yourself without having to be on your best behavior or "looking good." You can just sort of relax with yourself, because there is nothing you need to prove to yourself. You know yourself well, and this will come out in your portrait. And the wonder of self-portrait is that it can communicate so much more than simply what you look like.

For example, self-portrait can reveal your inner courage. The great Mexican artist Frida Kahlo not only captured her own likeness, she used self-portraits to express her feelings about life events, such as the polio that left one leg crippled. Through her cathartic, graphic portraits, she came to terms with injuries she sustained while a teenager, when a trolley car pierced her pelvis and required her to endure countless surgeries and continuous pain.

Frida Kahlo's self-portraits boldly declare her frank self-observation without judgment. There is no attempt to prettify or hide her imperfections. In many of her portraits she meticulously recorded her heavy eyebrows that appeared to form a single brow over both eyes. Sometimes she painted her eyebrows so that they looked like a blackbird in flight. She often included her mustache. Many of her self-portraits portray her wearing a long colorful skirt sweeping the floor, clothing peculiar to the Mexican Tehuantepec region. She lovingly recorded her slender waist and carefully plaited black hair, which she piled onto her head. She accentuated the positive and did not eliminate the negative; rather she bravely, defiantly, and brilliantly recorded what she saw in the mirror.

Frida's portraits are powerful depictions of everything that she wanted to record about herself. She captured her attire, physical traits, and actual life situations, including one painting of herself in a full body cast that she wore following an unsuccessful operation.

Self-portrait can also help you get in touch with and express your somber side, or perhaps express a sorrow you are feeling. The Dutch painter Rembrandt van Rijn, born in 1606, sketched his own face thousands of times and painted more than fifty self-portraits. Looking at his last portrait, painted just before his death at age sixty-three, we see a tired, heavy, wrinkled man, gazing at us with a defeated expression on his face. When I first saw this painting, I felt sad. He seems to ask us, "What does it all mean? Does it end like this?" Rembrandt himself said of his final portrait, "I came; it may be to look for myself and recognize myself. What have I found? Death painted I see ..."

It is interesting to note that Rembrandt never "judged" his failing body in his later portraits. Rather, it seems to me that he portrayed himself with a sense of objectivity, accurately rendering the effects of aging, such as wrinkles, drooping facial skin, and graying coarse hair.

He was brutally honest, carefully recording his changing emotions and aging features. In a 1961 book, art historian Manuel Gasser wrote, "Over the years, Rembrandt's self-portraits increasingly became a means for gaining self-knowledge, and in the end took the form of an interior dialogue: a lonely old man communicating with himself while he painted."

Or self-portraits can be playful, whimsical, and fun! We see this in the work of Marc Chagall. Born Mark Zakharovich Shagal, in 1887 in Belorussia (now Belarus), Chagall painted himself with a whimsical attitude. Chagall's self-portraits also depict biographical material, such as little villages, angels, lovers, flying cows, fiddlers, circus performers, and roosters. His paintings are lyrical poems that proclaim the beauty of all creation.

In his *Self-portrait with Seven Fingers*, a young man faces a canvas depicting a milkmaid and her cow. The canvas surface is fragmented, reflecting a Cubist influence, and we see symbols representing aspects of his life, including the Eiffel Tower and a hand holding a palette and brushes. The Eiffel Tower symbolized Chagall's love of French painting and the debt he felt he owed to Paris. We also can observe that Chagall did not "judge" himself as he portrayed himself, rather he revealed his emotions and interests and the loves and influences that shaped his life. He practiced self-observation without judgment.

I LOOK IN THE MIRROR AGAIN

I haven't painted a self-portrait since I was thirty-four years old, when I gazed into a round mirror and worked hard to get "a likeness" by capturing the sheen in my hair and the texture of the flannel shirt I was wearing. I was looking to truthfully reproduce what I saw in the mirror.

As I gaze into the mirror now, as I write, I observe a face that is very much like the one I remember from years ago, with a few changes. Some lines in my forehead and around my mouth, a different chin with some loose skin hanging below my jaw line. I also see my familiar brown eyes, a very familiar nose, and ears that look just like those in my baby pictures.

As I study my face in the mirror, pondering how I want to do a new self-portrait, I feel a little like I'm returning to a neighborhood I once lived in, which has changed but is still familiar. The streets are more broken up, with more cracks, but the buildings are sturdy and well built. There's no mistaking the neighborhood. There's something poignant about that, and beautiful too, which I want to express.

I am deciding what medium will best express the reality of what my eyes are seeing in the mirror. I am thinking about using pastels, because I want to record everything my eyes observe, and I can do this best with that medium. In the way that Rembrandt and Kahlo painted, I want to tell the truth without judging what I see.

Picasso said, "If only we could pull out our brain and use only our eyes." His words remind artists to trust our eyes unclouded by judgment. The brain, which Picasso wants to eliminate, is the organ that tends to limit our expression by judging, analyzing, evaluating, and criticizing everything it sees. The judging qualities of the mind must be quieted to allow us to observe, simply observe. The French painter Paul Gauguin echoed the importance of observation when he said, "I made a promise to keep a watch over myself, to remain master of myself, so that I might become a sure observer."

GETTING READY

How do you begin a self-portrait and what will you express? Picasso said, "Are we to paint what's on the face, what's inside the face, or what's behind it?" Good question! What would you want to express about yourself in your portrait?

If you want it to look *like* you, you will need to make the details accurate. If you don't care about a likeness, you can play with exaggerated proportions for fun. What mood do you want your self-portrait to convey?

Are there any personal objects such as jewelry or pieces of clothing you want to include? Any religious or spiritual symbols or images? If so, gather them together now.

Are there deeper themes you want to explore, a traumatic event you want to express? Or is there some part of you that you have strong feelings about and want to learn to observe with nonjudgment? How could these be expressed? Consider using colors that have symbolic or personal meaning.

Before beginning the body-centered experience, prepare your studio space for the art project. Carefully arrange a mirror on a tabletop or other place so you can comfortably observe yourself closely in it while painting. Gather any objects you want to include in your painting, and wear the clothes you will paint yourself wearing. Tape your paper to a backing board with a cushiony layer of newspaper in between, and gather your pastels and other supplies nearby.

LET'S CONNECT WITH OUR BODY AND BREATH

A wonderful way to show compassion and acceptance to yourself is to give your face a gentle massage. By stroking your eyes, cheeks, jaw, temples and scalp, you invite tight or sore muscles to relax, and you begin a process of self-observation that will accompany you as you begin your self-portrait. As you proceed, remember Swami Kripalu's words about practicing self observation without judgment.

Note: Before you begin the body-centered experience, read through the instructions several times until you are familiar with them and can proceed without referring to the book, or consider recording the directions to play back as you practice the face massage. This face massage is very relaxing and almost performs itself. Enjoy!

1. Sit on a couch or chair and remove your glasses, if you wear them. Rub your palms together very quickly for about one minute, or until you feel heat building in your hands. Place your palms against your eye sockets and feel the warmth penetrating into your eyes.

2. As you begin your massage, breathe steadily and allow your fingers to explore your face with love and compassion. Consciously let go of judgments as they arise, and return to your breath.

3. Rest your palms on your cheeks and massage your eyes through your closed lids with your middle and index fingers. Make small, gentle circles, and press gently into the eyelids and the entire bony area surrounding the eye. Linger on any area that is tender and needs some extra care. Explore the ridges of your eyebrows, and press the eye sockets right next to the bridge of the nose.

4. Massaging in gentle little circles, move your fingers inch by inch up to your forehead and across to your temples. Observe the sensations of your fingers encountering the bones and flesh. If your mind wanders into judgments about your face, bring your attention back to observing yourself touching your face. Return to your breath.

5. Massage your way slowly around your face. Feel the structure of bone and muscle in your cheeks, nose, and jaw. Observe the softness of your lips. Explore the nooks and crannies of your ears. Don't forget to use your fingernails to scratch your scalp!

6. If you encounter any sore places, simply press on the spot for a few seconds, breathing into the pain to release tension and pressure.

7. Spread your fingers wide and massage your whole head and scalp, moving your thumbs to the bottom of the skull, just above the neck. With your fingers resting on the top of your head, and elbows out to the side, gently yet firmly knead your thumbs into the space where the bottom of the skull meets the neck. In this position, you can feel your entire skull encased in your hands.

8. If you like, rub your hands together once again to create more heat, and spend some time massaging your neck and shoulders.

When you are finished, sit quietly for a while, allowing your breath to flow smoothly, and reflect on what you just experienced. Notice any thoughts, feelings, or memories that come to you, and let go of judgment. When you work on your self-portrait and need to take a break, repeat this exercise to help you tune in to yourself. If you like, write in your pad or notebook any insights that you gained.

Remember that you just performed a preliminary study of your face during the massage exercise. Try to sustain the insights and feelings you received during the experience and apply it to your painting project. During this massage, did you experience observation without judgment? If so, use this skill in your portrait.

LET'S PAINT!

As you begin to paint your self-portrait, return again to Swami Kripalu's words about self-observation without judgment. Look carefully in the mirror and have compassion for yourself. Let your portrait unfold slowly and enjoy the process. Celebrate the beauty in your facial features, your hair, everything that is beautiful and wonderful about you!

Remember also that your portrait doesn't have to be an exact likeness. Is there something besides how you look that you want to express—an attitude about life or an important personal belief? Don't be afraid to express what lies in your soul, and if a judgment creeps up, just return to the painting.

Note: The materials list and instructions for painting your self-portrait are for using pastels. However, if you are adventurous, you can also use alternative formats, such as watercolor, collage, batik, or any other medium you like. I have also included a few tips to consider if you create your self-portrait with a medium other than pastels.

Painting Your Self-Portrait

THINGS YOU WILL NEED

• *Large mirror that you can sit close to while painting*

• *Box of soft pastels, at least 36 colors (more colors are better)*

• *Vine charcoal*

• *Pastel paper*

• *Thick stack of newspaper to cushion your paper (insert between the paper and the backing board)*

• *Workable fixative (optional)*

• *Lamp or spotlight to illuminate your face (optional)*

Self-Portrait by Laura Riegelhaupt
(see color insert).

MAKING PRELIMINARY DECISIONS

First make some decisions about how you want your portrait to look.

1. Look at your face in the mirror. Immediately notice what thoughts, feelings, and judgments arise. Are you embarrassed by something? Do you like what you see? You can overcome judgment by noticing it when it comes up and then releasing it.

2. Observe your features and the colors you see in your skin, lips, eyes, and hair. What kind of self-portrait do you want to paint? If you have a strong-featured face, you may wish to create a bold portrait that looks solid and three-dimensional. If you have a sense of humor, consider painting a portrait with skewed proportions or that includes funny clothing or objects. Do you want to include only

your face, or part of your torso, too? How do you want to express *you*?

3. Notice the space around your body and face. What room are you in? What is on the walls? Are there windows? This negative space, or background, is also part of the portrait.

4. Pick a position for your face that will stay steady throughout the whole process. Will you paint a frontal view, with your face looking straight out at the viewer? Or will you do a three-quarter view? Gaze in the mirror to decide which view is most appealing.

BLOCKING IN YOUR FEATURES

The next step is to lightly sketch in your features with vine charcoal.

1. Use vine charcoal to begin your portrait by sketching the outline of your face and body. Use light strokes as you explore the general shape of your face and the line of your neck. Take your time.

2. After sketching the outline, fill in the general proportions of your features by lightly sketching in your eyes, nose, and mouth. Use your eyes to approximate distances between your features. If you want a more accurate likeness, consider sketching light horizontal and vertical lines through your face to aid in measuring. For example, draw a horizontal line through the eyes, extending the line across the page. This will help you gauge the best vertical placement of your ears.

3. Try to notice everything—the shape of your eyes, how high your forehead is, the curve of your lips. Observation is important every step of the way.

4. Keep observing your experience without judgment, and practice being the *witness* to your process of creation. If you are judging your performance, simply witness that judgment

THE PAINTING PATH

process. It is only a thought in your mind, and you can choose another thought in the next moment. Witness your ability to observe yourself without judgment.

BUILDING UP YOUR PORTRAIT

When you have the general shape and positions of your features blocked in, you are ready to start building up your portrait in increments by adding color.

1. If you want to create a more dynamic portrait, put a bright lamp to one side of your face as you draw. The light helps define the features; it creates shadows and a strong pattern of light and dark. It also emphasizes the solidity and three-dimensional quality of your features.

2. Choose a dark pastel and a light pastel to block in the dark and light shapes you see in the mirror. Two values of the same color work well for this—for example, a cream or beige color for lighter areas and a darker brown for the shadows. (Avoid black as your dark, as it will appear too harsh.) Also choose a very light color pastel, such as white or a light cream color, for highlighting the lightest areas you see.

3. Use your dark and light pastels to sketch and shade in the lightest and darkest places on your face. Notice where shadows fall. Use the sides of the pastels to apply a soft blanket of color to the planes of the face, including cheeks and forehead. Use the edges to create fine details.

4. As you fill in the extremes of light and dark, begin noticing what other colors you see in your face and their relative values, and gradually include those colors. For example, try to see the colors hidden within your skin. Do you see bronze or golden tones? Or maybe there are pinks or oranges? Keep observing without judgment.

159

But Does It Look Like Me?

5. Next, look deeper. You may be surprised by the colors you discover, such as reds and gold in your hair and perhaps pinks, blues, and even greens in your skin. Whatever you see, trust it without judgment. Gradually add each of these colors, and soon you will have a vibrant self-portrait.

When you are done, step back and look over your self-portrait with compassion. What do you see? If you see an area or detail that you want to develop more, go ahead, but don't overwork your picture. If you can't stand your self-portrait, let go of that judgment and simply do another one. Remember, that Rembrandt painted over sixty self-portraits! Frida Kahlo and Vincent van Gogh also could not stop looking in the mirror.

A self-portrait is a means of self-exploration as well as self-expression. You have joined the ranks of those who are willing to look within; the soul-searchers, the compassionate ones. May this be the first of many self-portraits you will paint, and may you continue to look at yourself with compassion and mercy. Swami Kripalu reminds us, "As long as we fail to enter the inner chamber of our heart, objective self-observation is not possible." Painting a self-portrait can lead you to the inner chamber of your heart, wherein lies compassion, mercy, and love.

Reflections

Take time to integrate your experience by writing in your notebook or journal. Write any insights you may have. Use the following questions and phrases to help to explore and clarify your thoughts. Write in your journal, notebook, or on a separate sheet of paper.

What do you judge harshly about yourself?

What do you see when you look into the mirror?

What did you learn about yourself by painting your self-portrait?

What does compassion mean to you?

Are you compassionate with yourself?

What quality do you admire most about yourself?

When I massaged my face I felt …

Every time I look in the mirror I …

If I accepted everything about myself …

The only thing that stops me from … is …

When I see myself with the eyes of … I know …

10 LISTENING TO OUR INTUITION

NURTURING COURAGE THROUGH OIL PAINTS

To thine own self be true …
And it must follow, as the night the day,
Thou can not then be false to any man.
—WILLIAM SHAKESPEARE

Van Gogh once wrote that "painting is a faith, and it imposes the duty to disregard public opinion." What he was talking about was what today we might call a gut feeling or intuition, having faith that the path you see is the right one for you, whatever others may have to say about it. Intuition is a knowing, a kind of personal guidance system that advises us. It's not based on reasoning or logic, but arises in a flash, bringing a message that may seem to make no sense, yet compels us to listen.

Artists in particular tend to have a strong sense of intuition—but this might not be the blessing that it first may appear to be, for our sense of direction often takes us in directions counter to prevailing opinions and tastes. Yet, in order to create and grow, we painters need to learn to hear, trust, and follow our intuition. We must learn to distinguish our own true inner voice from the voices around us, which may not understand our inner process, intentions, or motivations for creating our work.

This takes courage. In this chapter, we'll learn to follow our intuition with courage, first through a breathing exercise called breath of joy that expands the lungs and increases the oxygen in our system, then by exploring the bold medium of oil paints.

EVERYBODY'S A CRITIC

There are many external voices and obstacles to trusting our intuition and letting our creativity flow out, unhindered and unedited. Some of these voices come from people we know, love, and trust. My students frequently tell me stories about how, after a teacher or friend (often unintentionally) makes discouraging or insensitive remarks about their art, they return to their painting unsure of what to do. The words of these respected people sting and, when taken to heart, block access to our intuition.

Sometimes, the worst kind of criticism is what's *not* said! When I was a young high school art teacher, I displayed my recent work in the teachers' lounge, a series of large canvases I had painted while living and studying in Mexico. The expressive quality of these works reflected the influence of some of my teachers, portraying wild and crazy imagery. The canvases showed suggestive body parts such as thighs, faces, arms, and bellies that floated in a surrealistic atmosphere of experimental color harmonies. There were some realistic figures and others that were more abstracted and fragmented. The images were not ordinary, to say the least. My colleagues commented politely, calling my work "interesting" and "unusual." But they looked at me like I was from Mars! And who knows what they said when I wasn't in the room. There was no outright rejection of the work, but the smirks, raised eyebrows, and dumbfounded expressions discouraged me. It took courage for me to paint and then display those images, and when it was met with indifference, confusion, and scorn, I felt my courage melt away.

Perhaps if I had painted some docile landscapes, I would have won their approval. But pretty pictures were not what I was painting at age twenty-three. I was exploring every form of painting possible and learning from artists who had let go of "right doing and wrong doing." In time, I learned to recover my courage, listen to my intuition, and follow it. The writer Erica Jong could have been describing my experience when she wrote, "Everyone has talent. What is rare is the courage to follow the talent into the dark place where it leads."

THE INNER CRITIC

Another and often more powerful obstacle to following our intuition with courage is our own inner critic, which is usually fueled by some belief revolving around fear or doubt.

When I was a child and found myself wrestling with problems or decisions, my mother often advised me to be true to myself. I was fortunate in that regard, to have a parent who counseled me to listen to and heed my intuition. Unfortunately, being true to myself often seemed to go against what *I believed* others, including my mother, expected of me. My belief had nothing to do with reality, yet I had to fight against my own inner critic that insisted that, despite what my mother said, somehow following my own inner guidance would only result in failure, shame, and regret.

Here's an example of what I mean. Not long after I showed my paintings in the teachers' lounge at the high school where I taught, I began to feel an inner urge to leave my job. Every day it became harder to go to work and teach art to disinterested students. I began to yearn for the glorious year I took off to study art in Mexico, painting, weaving, doing batik, and generally living soulfully and making art all the time. Over time, I developed a strong urge to move to the West Coast with some friends, where we dreamed we could start a new, more authentic life of getting back to the land and doing art.

My intuition was guiding me, but I struggled with the decision. My inner critic nagged: What would I do about money? This was an important question, of course, but for me it became not a simple question to be answered but a nagging fear of what my mother, for whom money was very important, would think of me. She was proud of my being a high school art teacher and proud that I had a steady income. How would she feel about my quitting my secure profession and moving to Oregon with my friends to try and sell art for a living? Her advice was always that I should follow my intuition, but my *belief* that she would disapprove undermined my courage. I really wrestled with this dilemma until, finally, I found the courage to move and make art my livelihood. I'm so glad I did, because it turned out to be a real turning point in my life. I learned that living life on my own terms was a brave way to be, especially when some decisions flew in the face of common sense and security. But I could only follow the path that seemed right for me. As I learned to trust my intuition and ignore my inner critic, I learned to trust myself, and gained courage. Confucius said, "To know what is right and not to do it is the worst cowardice." Boy, was he right!

HOW DO YOU NURTURE YOUR COURAGE?

Eleanor Roosevelt once said something that may explain why I have learned to trust my intuition by being courageous. "We gain strength and courage and confidence by each experience in which we really stop to look fear in the face ... we must do that which we think we cannot."

In other words, we gain strength and courage by showing up and doing what we or others believe we can't because we don't have the talent or intelligence or skills. It doesn't matter how well or poorly we do it—success is not the goal. The goal is the experience itself.

I have found that this principle has played itself out over and again in my life. Was I terrified of taking a test? I'd show up and take it anyway. Regardless of the grade I received, I found that the next time I had to take a test, I was a little less fearful. Each time I overcame a fearful thought or did something that terrified me, I gained new confidence in my abilities. This has actually became a habit with me: When I find something daunting, I immediately try my hand at it.

This is how we nurture our courage, because after a while we realize that fear is just a thought and nothing more. It appears to have power over us, but the only real power it has is that which we voluntarily give it.

Painting from our intuition takes guts, courage, and fortitude. Applying the paint means we must engage and defeat our inner critic, and sharing our art with others means confronting opinions and voices of onlookers, both supportive and nonsupportive. But the more we do it, the more natural courage becomes to us.

WHY OIL PAINTING?

Working with oil paints is different than other media such as watercolor and pastel because they are gutsy, thick, and creamy. I love pastels, watercolors, and batik, but for me oil is the pinnacle of all painting media. Oil

paints are big and bold, and for that reason they take courage to use. They are not for the faint of heart.

Oil paints are also endlessly flexible. Artists throughout the ages have used them to convey every conceivable topic in every conceivable style, from awe-inspiring religious paintings by Renaissance artists like Titian and Tiepolo to the tradition-breaking experiments by the European Surrealists and the American Abstract Expressionist painters. Especially compelling to me are the daring works of Cézanne, Picasso, and the Cubists, who used the flexibility of oils to step outside tradition and convention. They began to break up the picture plane, fragmenting objects and rearranging them. They opened the door to all kinds of new expression including collage, abstraction, and minimal art. These artists didn't heed the rules. Instead, they listened to their own inner guidance, despite critical voices that ridiculed their daring inventions. These rule-breakers produced some of the world's greatest art.

The nineteenth-century French painter Cézanne opened the door for Cubism by presenting different vantage points within his still lifes and landscapes. By shifting our perspective within the painting, he suggested multiple views of the same scene, leading to the Cubist techniques of fragmenting objects and rearranging reality within the picture plane.

In the way that Cézanne shifted the perspective of his subjects, allow yourself to do the same in the following painting projects. Trust your intuition and let go of old concepts that prevent you from experiencing the present moment.

Cézanne himself sums up the painter's task in these words, "Right now a moment is fleeting by! Capture its reality in paint! To do that we must put all else out of our minds. We must become that moment, make ourselves a sensitive recording plate. Give the image of what we actually see, forgetting everything that has been seen before our time." The kernel of wisdom in Cézanne's words is that until we as artists have the courage to be in the moment when we paint and to let go of painting concepts that would keep us bound to the past, we will not truly be painting with courage and intuition. By making ourselves a "sensitive recording plate," he encourages us to trust what our eyes see, however we might see it. He guides us to erase from our mind images, clichés, and concepts that are familiar and secure. By heeding his advice, we may courageously following our intuition.

This is similar to Krishnamurti's concept of "choiceless awareness," in which we confront each moment unhindered by beliefs, prejudices, and concepts. It's also akin to Suzuki Roshi's beginner's mind, in which we let ourselves approach life with an attitude of not knowing and experience each moment as it is.

GETTING READY

The art project for this chapter involves painting the human figure. Take some time to leaf through magazines or catalogs, looking for images of people in different positions such as walking, pointing, sitting, dancing, or playing. Cut out several pictures of figures that you find interesting.

Set up a large table in front of you with the materials you will need to begin your oil-painting project, including your easel, palette, paints, and brushes. Remember to cover with newspaper any surfaces you want to protect from paint drips. When you are ready, move into the body-centered experience.

Listening to Our Intuition

LET'S CONNECT WITH
OUR BODY AND BREATH

The breathing exercise known as the breath of joy is a yogic breath that expands three sections of the lungs: the abdominal (bottom), thoracic (middle), and clavicular (upper) areas. As you move your arms into different positions in conjunction with your breathing, you oxygenate portions of the lungs that everyday shallow breathing does not.

This breathing exercise cleanses the lungs of carbon dioxide, toxins, and stale air and brings fresh oxygen to the lungs, bloodstream, and cells throughout the body. It also releases tension, opens a flow of energy through the body, and clears cobwebs from the mind.

I have found breath of joy to be an excellent way to open energy channels and allow creativity to flow out with power and confidence. It is the perfect exercise for developing courage and confidence and to nurture you intuitive voice.

The movements are quick in the breath of joy, so move your arms in a lively manner when performing the different steps, as if you were a conductor leading an orchestra in a lively rendition of "Stars and Stripes Forever" or "Oklahoma!" It takes a little time to get used to the synchronization of breath with movement, but once you get it, it is enlivening.

Note: Read the instructions several times to become familiar with the arm movements and how they are coordinated with the breathing. Feel free to read the instructions into a tape recorder and play them back as you perform the movements and breathing.

1. Stand with your feet hip-width apart and bend your knees slightly. Put a gentle smile on your face and think of inviting in positive energy, courage, and intuition. Visualize yourself doing this exercise, inhaling to gradually expand your lungs' capacity to hold oxygen, and exhaling to release stale energy, carbon dioxide, toxins, and tension.

2. Swing your arms in front of you, so they rise up to be parallel to the floor. Fling them up energetically rather than slowly lifting. As you fling them up, inhale about one-third of your lung capacity. Don't worry about which part is being filled, just leave some room for more air to come in. The inhalation will feel a little like sniffing in air, with a quick, short "sniff."

3. Next, swing your arms to the side of your body, like a bird in flight, keeping them at shoulder height. There's a graceful little curve to the movement as you extend them to the side, like a conductor would do. As you move your arms in this direction, inhale more air, this time filling the lungs about one-third more. Again, sniff the air energetically.

4. Finally, raise your arms over your head toward the ceiling without clasping them, as if someone said, "Reach for the sky!" As you raise your arms skyward, take in the last bit of oxygen to fill your lungs to their full capacity. In this position, your chest should be completely expanded with lots of air.

5. During your three inhalations of air, use a single long, inhaling breath lasting throughout all three arm movements. As you synchronize your arms with the inhalations, you may feel like your arms are doing a little dance. These three arm positions are perfectly designed to fill the lungs completely. Again don't concern yourself with which part of the lungs gets filled. Your body will do it on its own.

6. Bend your knees, then bend your torso forward, bringing your chest toward your knees. With your mouth open, expel all the air you just inhaled in one giant exhalation and make the sound *ha* (loudly if you like). As you lean forward, bend your knees as much as is comfortable for your

169

Listening to Our Intuition

body. At the same time, fling your arms back behind you, as if you were about to dive into an imaginary swimming pool. Connect this arm movement with the first three that you practiced, so that the movements feel like a dance of your arms.

7. Repeat these movements three times, or more, if you have the inclination. If you notice that you feel out of breath, rest in between each round of inhalations and exhalations. You may feel a little lightheaded after a couple of rounds of breath of joy. This is because you have introduced more air into your lungs than you are used to. This is a good exercise to do anytime you need a little extra energy.

Another exercise to encourage intuition is simply to dance! Put on some of your favorite music and let your body move any way it wants to in rhythm to the music. I happen to love dancing to Aretha Franklin's "Respect" and Marvin Gaye's "I Heard It through the Grapevine." You can also develop courage by putting on music you don't normally listen to—reggae, for example, if you are a classical music fan—and letting your body again discover how it wants to express itself to the music. Dancing to music is also fun to do while you are painting: it keeps the creativity flowing and the energy high.

LET'S PAINT!

For many years, I believed that only way to paint with oils was to use genuine oil paints that thin with turpentine and mix with linseed oil. About ten years ago, I discovered that using water-based oil paints provides a lot of advantages over "real" oil paints, such as their being odorless and easy to clean up with soap and water. At the same time, they have the firm and juicy texture of oil-soluble paints, and they remain wet for several days, allowing you to rework the wet canvas to eliminate or add details. I get similar results and have the same amount of fun, with less hassle.

Exploring Oil Paints Using Color-Mixing and Palette Knife

THINGS YOU WILL NEED

WATER-BASED OIL PAINTS

• One tube each of the three primary colors: cadmium yellow, ultramarine blue, and alizarin crimson (or other shades of yellow, blue, and red)

• One tube each of titanium white and ivory black

• Additional optional colors: Naples yellow, pthalo blue, sap green, yellow ochre, burnt sienna, cadmium red, cerulean blue, lemon yellow, raw sienna

BRUSHES

• ½-inch bristle brush (stiff brush usually made of hog hair)

• 1-inch sable brush (very smooth brush, good for blending)

• 1-inch synthetic sable brush, less expensive than real sable

• 1-inch bristle brush

• 2-inch filbert oil painting brush (a rounded brush that can make wide or narrow strokes; good for blending)

• 2-inch chip brush from hardware store

• Two 3-inch bristle brushes

• Palette knife

• Several different sizes of filberts or rounds for oil painting (optional)

MISCELLANEOUS

• *1 or 2 stretched canvases, at least 20 by 24 inches (the larger the better)*

• *Disposable palette made of coated paper with tear-off sheets, at least 11 by 14 inches (the larger the better)*

• *Several colorful magazines or catalogs*

• *Scissors*

• *Cotton and terry-cloth rags*

• *Large coffee can or plastic jar for water*

• *Masking tape*

• *Small jar of water-soluble linseed oil (optional) and small plastic container to hold it*

• *Small jar of water- soluble stand oil (optional) and with small plastic container to hold it*

• *Vine charcoal*

• *Smock, apron, or old clothes that can get dirty*

• *Easel for your canvas (table or standing)*

• *Newspaper to cover your work table (optional; plastic cover is fine too)*

• *Brown wrapping paper, Kraft paper*

• *Workable fixative (like the kind you used for pastels)*

Using Your Intuition to Mix Oil Paints

In chapter 3, we learned how to mix watercolors, but mixing oil paint is a different experience altogether. Oil paints have a way about them. From the moment you squeeze the paint out of the tubes, you will be entering a world of luscious, rich colors and thick pigments. With their buttery, full-bodied consistency, they seem to speak to something in your soul. They are ideal for encouraging you to delve deep into your memories, experience, and intuition and to explore the richness of colors.

Knowing how much fun oil painting is, our first step will be to make a really big palette by placing two sheets of your disposable palette paper next to each other, giving you plenty of room to mix to your heart's content. In my experience, I always need more mixing room than I think I will.

1. Tape at least two palette sheets to the newspaper-covered table.

2. Begin with your tubes of ultramarine blue, alizarin crimson, and cadmium yellow. With these three primary colors, as well as white and black, you'll be mixing a myriad of delicious colors. Use your intuition and be brave.

3. Squeeze a blob of color from each tube onto your palette. The blobs should be about the size of a half-dollar. Position them on your palette in a triangular shape, with each color at the point of the triangle. Leave about four inches between the colors.

4. Use the tip of the palette knife to pick up a portion of yellow paint and put it on the palette in a clean spot. Clean the knife on a rag. (Clean the knife frequently to keep your colors pure.)

5. Next, dig into the red paint with your knife, remove a tiny bit, and mix it with the yellow you've separated from the original blob. Push the paint in all directions until you've created a well-mixed glob of the secondary color, orange, with no streaks. If the orange looks too similar to the red, add a little more yellow to your mixture. Trust your intuition and mix as long as you like to get the color you are looking for.

6. Repeat this process with red and blue to create another secondary color, purple. Experiment with your palette knife,

Listening to Our Intuition

blending your colors with strength and energy until there are no streaks. Stay in tune with your intuition, and when you have a nice purple that you like, keep it. Mixing directly with your palette knife allows you to combine the colors thoroughly and to form separate piles of gorgeous color.

7. Repeat the process with yellow and blue to mix the final secondary color, green.

8. Squeeze out a blob of titanium white on one side of your palette. Use your palette knife to create new mixtures of color by combining white with the six other colors you have (three primary and three secondary). When white is mixed with a color, it creates a tint of that color. Adjust the amount of white and color you combine until you have the tints that you want.

9. Squeeze out a blob of black onto your palette. This time, use a one-half-inch or one-inch bristle brush to combine it with your many colors to create shades of those colors. How many different shades can you create? (Clean your brush frequently.) Don't forget to mix black and white to create various shades of gray. If you feel very courageous, combine gray with the primary and secondary colors to come up with some truly surprising and luscious colors.

10. By now, your palette should be bursting with exotic color mixtures. Some are beautiful, and others may look like mud. But sometimes mud is exactly the right color to paint with to set off contrasting colors. The color mud next to a bright turquoise makes it sing! Have the courage to paint with mud if your intuition guides you to do so.

11. Open the water-soluble stand oil and the linseed oil. Pour a little linseed oil into one small plastic container and a little stand oil mixed with some water into another small plastic container.

Using Intuition and Courage to Paint the Human Figure

Consider the many ways the human figure has been painted throughout history: Cave painters painted primitive figures stalking animals, Renaissance artists used dramatic light and shadow to render the human figure realistically, and abstract painters dissected and fragmented the figure to show different viewpoints of the figure and its environment. Allow yourself to tune in to your intuition. Be courageous and paint the human figure as you see it, as your intuition guides you.

Serena, Jack, and Friends by Linda Novick (see color insert).

1. Cut a piece of brown Kraft paper to the size of your canvas. Take the images of human figures you cut from magazines, and play with arranging them on the paper. Move the figures around until you find a composition that appeals to you. Consider making them relate to one another in some way, perhaps through color (each wears something red), through action (maybe they appear to be gesturing to one another), or through shape (each has something triangular about them). Once your composition is set, glue or tape the figures onto the paper.

Step 1: Arrange images of human figures on Kraft paper (see color insert).

2. Use vine charcoal to transfer the outlines and details of your composition to your canvas, changing proportions as necessary and altering it in any way you see fit. This will be the basis of your painting. Do you want to make it realistic? Do you want to experiment with breaking the figures apart? Follow your intuition. If you need to make corrections to the charcoal

sketch, use a damp rag with soap and water to erase and redraw. When you are done, spray the sketch with fixative to keep the charcoal from smudging when you apply the paint.

Step 2: Use vine charcoal to transfer the outlines and details of the figures to your canvas.

3. Once the figures are on the canvas, the first step is to apply washes of color to block in basic areas of color. Doing this will show you what the colors will look like once you begin to apply the paint more thickly. Dip a two-inch bristle brush into a color and then into water. On a clean space on your palette, mix the paint thoroughly with the water until you have a fully loaded brush. Keep a rag in hand to wipe up any drips that you don't want.

Step 4: Block in basic areas of color with washes (see color insert).

4. Paint the wash on the canvas, either filling in one or more of the figures or using it for the background color. Continue using washes of different colors to establish a basic color scheme for your painting. Here is where you can really trust your intuition by choosing colors that you think look good together, regardless of what colors are in the original pictures. Use the colors you mixed that are most pleasing to your eye. The washes create a family of colors that you will follow, but they are open to change and invention at any time in the painting process.

5. Dip your brush into the linseed oil you put into the plastic container, touch the brush to a blob of color on the palette, and mix them well on the palette. Feel the creaminess of the oil and enjoy how it blends with the paint. Apply the paint and oil mixture to your canvas, feeling it glide on. Let yourself be absorbed in the process and let your intuition flow as you paint over the underpainting with details of the human figure as you see it.

6. Choose a new brush, or carefully clean the one you are using, and dip it into the stand oil and water mixture. Mix it with another color of paint and apply it to the canvas. How does it feel compared to painting with the linseed oil? It's OK to mix them together as they are totally compatible. Use the medium you like best, or use both. (Stand oil produces transparency and brightness and gives colors stiffness, gloss, and body.)

7. Continue building up your painting, using any combination of colors and paints (straight, or mixed with linseed or stand oil) as you want. Choose your colors by instinct rather than by what you think they should be. This exercise is about making choices based on intuition, not on logic or reason. Go with your gut feelings regardless of what anyone might say.

Here are some things to consider as your work on your painting:

- If you find an area of your painting that you don't like, remove the paint by first scraping it off with the palette knife and then using a wet rag to remove most of the paint. Once it dries, rework the area making any changes you wish to make.

- Think about repeating colors to lead your eye through the canvas.

- Your background or negative space can be a solid color, have assorted colors, or be a gradation of a single color, such as tints and shades of blue. Consider using a color that contrasts sharply with the colors in your figure to help make it stand out.

- If you are painting the figures in a more realistic fashion, remember to include shadows to create a three-dimensional quality to the figures.

Listening to Our Intuition

- If your figures overlap on your canvas, consider creating an illusion of transparency by painting the overlapping areas a third color. For example, if the blue arm of one figure overlaps the yellow leg of another figure, paint that shape green (blue plus yellow makes green).

- Be brave. Try new things as you trust your instincts and urges. Let go of needing to get it right. Try any techniques that occur to you, such as scratching into the paint with your knife to create lines. The technique of scratching into the top layer of paint is called *sgraffito* and can also be done using the tip of the brush handle.

- Take it in steps. Since oil paint takes a few days to dry, you can return to it on a different day to add something while it is still wet and workable.

When you have covered the whole canvas with color and you can't think of anything else to do, you are finished. Let it dry and return to it in a few days to behold what you've created.

Letting go of time-honored ways of doing things and well-known territory is the job of the painter. Doing and seeing things differently can be daunting and requires courage. Releasing clichéd concepts requires us to trust our intuition and gut reactions and develop courage. The great French painter Henri Matisse said, "There is nothing more difficult for a truly creative painter than to paint a rose, because before he can do so he has first to forget all the roses that were ever painted." It is a challenge to us all to forget what we know well and look with fresh eyes.

We nurture our intuition each time we dance like no one is watching, paint like there are no art critics, and cherish that still small voice that has always whispered in our ears. Each time you choose a color, sing a note, or embark on a new venture, remember that if you remain true to yourself, you will inspire others to follow their own truth. As you trust your intuition, you will inspire others to trust theirs.

Reflections

Take time to write some words in your journal or notebook that will help you clarify your ideas and integrate your experience. You can start with returning to your breath to center and focus yourself. When you are ready, you can complete the following questions and phrases. Add more writing if you are moved to do so.

Do you usually try to do things that are acceptable to other people and society at large?

How did you feel when you practiced the breath of joy?

What was your experience like when you did the color-mixing exercise?

What was most fun about the figure-painting project?

What was most challenging about that project?

The thing that stops me from enjoying painting is …

When I let go of … I could more easily …

I was really able to trust my intuition when it came to …

With this project I finally learned that …

11

THE STORIES WE TELL

REINTERPRETING OUR LIVES THROUGH PAINTED AUTOBIOGRAPHY

Spring unfolds anew …
Now in my second childhood
Folly, Folly, too

—ISSA

Artists excel at observation. We love to look deep into the heart of things and discover meaning. We love to make connections between things, often in ways that only visual artists can do. The more we practice our painting, the better we become at uncovering and expressing hidden emotions and deep truths about ourselves. From time to time, we may even believe we see behind the great curtain and catch a glimpse of the truth.

Yet, as we have discovered with some of our practices, such as witness consciousness, we do not always see things exactly as they are. Often we attach meaning, feelings, and impressions to things that have little to do with the things themselves but are rooted in our own mercurial thoughts and emotions.

Sometimes, the significance we attach to the facts and events of our lives takes the form of particularly powerful stories that we tell ourselves over and over. These stories often say more about our perceptions, decisions, and actions than they do about the events that sparked them. There is profound insight in the Roman emperor Marcus Aurelius's words, "A person's life is dyed with the color of his imagination"—that is, we see the facts and events of our lives through filters, which tint our perception and hence what we believe. These filters are our stories.

Unfortunately, these stories can often limit us in ways that we might not even realize, especially those stories that took root when we were very young. For some of us, those childhood stories are still running the show, determining our actions and reactions to this day. For example, a bad grade on a paper may have blossomed into the story "I'm not very smart," which could, even today, be preventing you from pursuing more education.

But, as the nineteenth-century Victorian novelist George Eliot once wisely said, "It is never too late to be what you might have been." We may understand her words to suggest that we "improve" our lives by taking some course of action, such as completing an unfinished graduate degree. But more importantly, these words suggest that we can fundamentally alter our lives by reinterpreting our stories in more empowering ways to create a new context from which to live our lives. In turn, this can help us begin to reclaim parts of ourselves that we have given up on.

In this chapter, we will reflect on the power of stories in our lives and how some of the stories we carry with us may, in fact, be unhelpful and untrue. Our body-centered experience centers on guided eye exercises designed to expand our vision. As you physically stretch your eyes beyond your normal range of movement, you will symbolically be stretching and expanding your inner vision, allowing you to witness yourself and your life story with flexibility, compassion, and *insight*. The art project is a visual autobiography that will give you the opportunity to dig into your own life and discover new and empowering interpretations of old stories, and thus influence the course your future will take. It does not have to be heavy and serious. You may find reasons to laugh at yourself and the ways you've viewed certain events in your life. Be open to discovery.

The form of your autobiography is up to you. You may even consider it a kind of graduation project, putting to use the skills and techniques you have learned or strengthened in this book. You will create your own materials list and also make some written plans for the project's execution.

WHAT IS A STORY, ANYWAY?

The Italian writer Umberto Eco wrote, "I have come to believe that the whole world is an enigma, a harmless enigma that is made terrible by our own mad attempt to interpret it as though it had an underlying truth." I love how he phrased his philosophy. When we try to analyze the inherent mystery of life, we impose a structure on something so mercurial that it defies simple categories and meanings.

I understand his words to mean that we humans often look at the mysteriously enigmatic facts and events of our lives and infuse those events with a certain meaning. We attempt to impose a structure on the inherent mystery of life, and this structure often takes the form of stories. That's what stories are: the personal embellishments and interpretations we layer over the simple, enigmatic facts of our lives. We tell our story throughout our lives to ourselves, confidantes, and even strangers. We create this story, and we begin to believe that it is true. The more we tell the story, the more we reinforce it in our minds until we are convinced that it is absolutely true. Whatever we say about our lives determines if we will feel fulfilled or unfulfilled, disappointed or grateful, angry or joyful. And, unfortunately, these stories are often erroneous and mistaken and limit us rather then empower us.

I USED TO BELIEVE THAT …

Stories that we begin to tell ourselves in childhood carry a particular power. Often, one defining moment in childhood can become much larger than the moment itself: it takes on potent meaning, a story that determines the spin that we will put on life events. Perhaps you wandered away from your mother in the grocery store and panicked. From that, you might tell yourself that the world is not a safe place. Maybe the event was less trivial—loss of a loved one, a move to a strange town, or the arrival of a sibling. How you interpreted that defining event often determines if you will see your life in a positive or negative light, as a painful struggle or an easy glide.

A story that I struggled with for years went like this: I am too big. I shared in a previous chapter that when I was seven years old, I looked at a photograph of my dancing partner and me. Her body was thin and lithe, and there was me, standing next to her, taller and bigger and heavier. I could have simply observed, without adding interpretation, that we had different body types. But, of course, it wasn't that simple. I knew immediately that something was wrong with me! Right away, even at seven years old, I gave the fact of our different sizes meaning—in this case, a highly negative one for me. I was too big!

A few years later, this story was reinforced in some powerful ways. First, during a routine doctor's examination, my doctor told my mother and me that I was overweight. He put me on a diet! This was powerful evidence that something was definitely wrong with me—and coming from no less an authority than a doctor!

Then, not long after that, a neighbor teased me by asking, "Hey, Linda, where are you wrestling on Saturday night?"—like I was some kind of lady wrestler. I was mortified and wanted to hide in my room for a week.

These events solidified the story in my mind, and I decided that I needed to change my body—I thought maybe I needed to change *me*. This set the trajectory for my lifelong battle with body image and body size. As a result, I found myself dieting to lose weight for most of my teenage and adult life.

Once we cross the line from observation to belief, we tend to collect evidence that further reinforces the supposed truth of the story and judgment. Even when we encounter clear, hard evidence that seems to be contrary to our story, we tend to discount it as erroneous or a fluke. In my teenage years and beyond, I met people who complimented me on my body. That was nice, but it did little to convince me that "I am too big" was, in fact, an erroneous story. Our stories can even become so ingrained in us that we come to depend on them: they are part of our identity, which only makes change that much more difficult. In time, these stories become part of a much larger belief system about ourselves in which we evaluate our actions and pronounce a sentence on ourselves. Often our sentence includes regret, shame, guilt, and disappointment.

What story have you told yourself throughout your life that you would like to change? Where and when did you first have the experience that became the basis for this story? You can probably remember a time when your story became reinforced, more solid and real. You believed it to be *true*. What happened? Did you hear critical words from family or friends? Did you experience rejection from someone you loved? Consider also the role your religion or faith may have played in reinforcing your story. Stories are often at the core of religious beliefs and have extraordinary power to reinforce our own stories, both positive and negative, about ourselves.

BUT NOW I SEE THAT ...

Many years later I had the opportunity to look through a box of old family photographs. I was struck by the pictures of myself at different ages—child, teen, young adult—because they didn't always match the image I had of myself of being too big.

One photograph in particular caught me by surprise. It was taken when I was in my early twenties and living in Mexico. There I am, a young woman, beautiful and voluptuous, buying a bag of strawberries from a fruit vendor in San Miguel. At first, I thought that couldn't be me—I never looked that good! But it was me, and as I stared at that photo, my mind was flooded with memories from one of the happiest times in my life, the time I lived in Mexico and studied painting and weaving at the local art school.

That discovery helped spark a process, including working with these images in a visual autobiography, by which I began to reinterpret my long-held story that "I am too big." I realized that the story was founded on certain data—the photo of me as a seven-year-old ballet dancer—but the story itself was a confused bundle of judgments, fears, and who knows what else. The story was essentially hollow and had no real power beyond what I had been giving it all those years. It's a little like that moment in *The Wizard of Oz* when Toto pulled the curtain back to reveal that the great and powerful Oz was nothing more than an insecure little man hiding behind some fancy technicolor pyrotechnics.

Of course, as you work with your own story, the process may not be simple. "Pay no attention to that man behind the curtain!" the great Oz thundered, trying to cling to the illusion of control, even after the jig was up. Likewise, our stories have a lot of residual influence that may be difficult to ignore. But if we are intentional, we can find new ways to interpret the data and empower our lives, instead of depleting them.

Here's the way I see my body now. I have always been a healthy, solid, and athletically built person. The nature of my body structure is compact, and I have broad shoulders and well-formed muscles. I have great agility, strength, and stamina. Among other benefits, my body allows me to be a fast swimmer and a good runner and skater—all things I love to do. I now see that my body is the perfect vehicle for me in this life. (Anyway, what's wrong with a lady wrestler?)

I feel sad when I think of how, for so many years, I judged my body and tried to make it conform to the image that I held in my mind. But I also have compassion for myself, realizing how powerful outside voices influenced my perception of my body. Otherwise, criticizing myself for succumbing to this story could become yet another story, namely, "I should have seen it another way!"

The content of your story may be different. We often regret the love affairs that ended, or the path not taken. My students share that they wished they had chosen to become artists when they were young and had more time to paint and create. Yet I believe that no experience we have had was a waste of time, and no choice we made at the time was wrong. Each and every event and experience we had went into making you who we are today.

We can rewrite our story from "I used to believe that ..." to "but now I see that ..." We can let go of our regret at not completing our degree, or of giving up a career as an actress to get married and raise children. By saying different things, changing the conversation, and cleaning our eye-glasses, we are free to see things in a new light.

WHY AUTOBIOGRAPHY?

We as artists can sense the power of creating this autobiography with each stroke of the brush. Frida Kahlo is an artist whose paintings are almost completely autobiographical. Through her beautifully blended vivid colors, she was able to reinterpret the traumatic events in her life. By painting the physical and emotional suffering she experienced, she came to terms with these events.

A visual autobiography helps you see your life from another point of view. You are looking back with new eyes, from this time in your life. The magic of this process is in reviewing and seeing: seeing how you have felt and seeing how you feel now.

In fact, whatever medium you choose, I suggest you consciously orient your autobiography around these two phrases:

I used to believe that ... but now I see that ...

For example, if the story you want to gain a new perspective on has to do with your own creativity, you might orient your autobiography around this statement: "I used to believe that my sister was the artist in the family, but now I see that I have creative gifts that she does not have." Thinking of your autobiography in this way will help it to be a dynamic spiritual exercise and not simply a time to reinforce negative stories or to reminisce about good times.

You may shed a few tears or have a hearty chuckle as you revisit the different chapters of your life. When you can see life's events as a story, you may see another point of view. In the same way that you invented the story, you can uncreate it or re-create it. You can let go of your usual form of suffering and bring back the "hour of splendor in the grass, glory in the flower." You can begin to write the next chapter of your life.

I still work on my autobiography from time to time, which is one of the beautiful things about it—as long as you are alive, you can continue to add to it. I especially like to make collages because it's fun working with old photographs—altering them by painting or cutting them—and I can add to it indefinitely without it ever feeling complete, on the one hand, or unfinished, on the other.

GETTING READY

Before beginning the following experience, take some time to gather what you will need to begin your autobiography project. If you are just beginning, you'll need only a pen and a notebook to plan the project and make a list of materials. If you've already completed the planning, then gather the art materials you will need to begin the artistic process.

 ## LET'S CONNECT WITH OUR BODY AND BREATH

Swami Sitaramananda once said, "The fastest way to bring the mind into concentration is through the eyes." The following exercises allow us to explore some eye movements that gently stretch and strengthen the muscles around the eyes. They also help relieve tension in the eye, increase blood flow to the optic nerve, and alleviate general stress and anxiety.

Note: Read through the instructions several times to familiarize yourself with them so you will not have to refer to the book as you are practicing this exercise. Alternatively, read the instructions into a tape recorder and then play them back as you proceed.

> 1. Sit comfortably in a chair and relax your body, placing your hands on your knees or thighs. Take a few minutes to center yourself by bringing all your attention to your breath. Allow your mind to become absorbed in the sensations of breathing. If thoughts about the past or the future arise, simply let them come and go.

2. When you feel centered, look straight ahead and imagine that you are looking at the face of a very large clock. Picture the different positions of the clock—twelve at the top, six at the bottom, nine and three at the sides, and so on.

3. Keep your spine erect but not rigid. Then, looking straight ahead and without lifting your head, move your eyes to gaze up at the twelve on the imaginary clock in front of you. Feel the stretch in your eye muscles. Look up only as far as feels comfortable. Hold this gaze for a moment, then lower your eyes to look down at the six at the bottom of the clock. Hold that gaze for a moment. Keep your head still and move your eyes up and down to gaze alternately at the twelve and the six. Repeat three or four times or until you feel the muscles getting tired. When you are finished, blink four or five times rapidly to release the tension in your eyes. Close your eyes and let them rest a moment.

4. Open your eyes and repeat this process by moving your eyes right and left to gaze alternately at the nine and the three on the sides of the imaginary clock. Feel the sensations of stretching the muscles of the eyes. Repeat at least three or four times or until you feel that the muscles are tired, and then blink quickly four or five times and close your eyes for a moment.

5. Repeat this process by looking from the imaginary one on the clock face diagonally down to the seven for several times, then from the eleven down to the five. Become aware of the sensations of stretching and simply notice how it feels to move your eyes in this way. Allow your breath to flow smoothly and regularly as you explore these movements.

6. Next, focus on the twelve at the top of the imaginary clock face. Hold your head stationary and slowly move your eyes clockwise around the face of the clock. Do several complete circuits, some slow and some fast. Blink your eyes a few times, then close them for a few seconds.

7. Now reverse direction and trace several counterclockwise circles around the clock face at different speeds. Then blink your eyes and rest them.

8. Finish this exercise by rubbing both palms together very quickly. When they are very hot, place your palms against your eyes and let the heat bathe your eyes in warmth. As your eyes drink in the warmth, focus on slow and steady breathing.

9. If you wish, gently massage your eyelids and eye sockets, moving your fingers in small circles, pressing any places that feel like they need a massage. Try using your thumbs to massage the sockets. Work your finger above the eyes to the brow and the temples. Enjoy the massage, while breathing smoothly, savoring the whole experience.

Take some time to relax before beginning to work on your art project. Allow the eye exercises to reverberate inside your head for a moment or two. Return your attention to your breath, and relax your body. Gradually transition from the eye movements and begin to think about your autobiography.

LET'S PAINT!

Congratulations! In the course of this book, you have learned or deepened your skills in a wide variety of art projects and painting techniques. This final project is the culmination of everything that has come before, and the specific form of this final project is up to you. Did you especially love working with watercolors? Then this can be a watercolor project. If you can't wait to do more resist, or another batik, here is your chance. You can even combine techniques. Anything goes!

But whatever medium you choose, let your project revolve around two distinct parts that represent the transformation of your personal story. The first part will represent the story as you used to know it. How you express it is up to you; it could be as literal as one-half of your painting labeled "I used to believe that ..." The second part will represent how you understand that story today. Again, it could be as clear as labeling the other half of your painting, "But now I see that ..." Taken together, these two parts will express the transformation of an old, limiting story into an empowering new interpretation.

Following are the general steps to take for creating an autobiography of your own making.

Using Painting to Tell Your Story

STEP 1: CHOOSE A STORY YOU WANT TO REINTERPRET

What stories do you have in your soul that trouble you? This event or incident can be something that you have thought about a lot over the course

A Brief Bittersweet Autobiography by Linda Novick (see color insert).

of your life—a specific regret, disappointment, trauma, or harsh judgment. Alternatively, you can explore a story that brings you great joy and express it so that you can find more things about it to celebrate, such as the day you got your pilot's license or the day you gave birth to your first child. It doesn't have to be all doom and gloom! Nevertheless, I have found that this way of working with painful memories can bring healing and hope.

Begin by listing several possible stories that you would like to explore. Write them all down and then choose one. If you have trouble coming up with ideas, feel free to use the prompts below to generate some thoughts.

I can't forgive myself for …

My parents were … which caused me to …

If I could live any day of my life over, it would be the day that …

I still cringe when I think of …

One of my favorite memories is the time that …

When you have your list, narrow it down to a single story, so that your project will have a distinct focus. Which one do you want most to see transformed, or to at least view with a different interpretation? Which would make an interesting art project? Which can you envision being expressed with the materials you want to use for this project?

If the story you choose is one that you have already transformed in your mind, then creating an art project around it can be a wonderful way to deepen your new interpretation. If it is a story that you still struggle with, this art project can be the means by which you find new ways of seeing that old story.

STEP 2: PLAN THE FORM OF YOUR AUTOBIOGRAPHY

Your next step is to write about how you see your autobiography taking shape. Take some time to really envision the project. Let it unfold in your mind, taking note of colors you want to use, objects you want to include, and anything else that comes to mind. Will you combine two or more media? If so, how? Use beginner's mind and approach both your story and the project with wonder and curiosity. Write down all your thoughts and ideas without editing them. Later, you can identify the ideas that will work best for this project and save the others for later.

Write down the theme for your autobiography, "I used to believe that … but now I see that …" If you aren't able to fill in the second part of that sentence yet, don't worry. This project itself can be a way of discovering how that sentence should end.

STEP 3: CREATE AN ACTION PLAN AND A LIST OF MATERIALS

Next, review your notes and write out a clear, step-by-step action plan in which you detail the specific steps you will need to take to put your project together. These will resemble the step-by-step instructions found in the projects throughout this book, and they should include all the materials you will need. It is important to plan carefully, because there's nothing more frustrating than being absorbed in a project, only to discover you are missing a vital color, brush, or other material because you forgot to note it! When your step-by-step list is complete, distill it down into a shopping list of the materials you will need, and then obtain any materials you don't already have.

STEP 4: CREATE YOUR AUTOBIOGRAPHY

When you have all the materials needed for your project, select your favorite body-oriented experience from this book and practice it again. When you are ready, begin creating your autobiography, following the step-by-step action plan you created yourself. Let the project take as many hours, days, or weeks as you need. If the story you are exploring is one that has not been transformed, allow this to be a time and space where you let your mind wander, looking for new ways of understanding that story.

STEP 4: WORDS HAVE POWER

Depending on the medium you are using for your autobiography, including actual words in your project may seem out of place. Yet the stories we rehearse and repeat to ourselves over and over are composed of words, even if only in our own minds. The actor James Earl Jones once said, "One of the hardest things in life is having words in your heart that you can't utter." "Uttering" those words by including them in this particular project can have an especially powerful effect on the psyche.

If you are tempted to explore the power of words, I encourage you to go for it and let your intuition guide you. For example, you could label the first part of your autobiography, "I used to believe that …" and the second part, "But now I see that …" Such words are a declaration in your project. A strong declarative statement can affect us deeply, as witnessed by the Declaration of Independence, or in Genesis 3: "And God said, 'Let there be light: and there was light.'" These examples powerfully demonstrate how declarations can transform countries, worlds, and universes. What would you like to declare about yourself?

If you do add words, consider the many ways you can incorporate them.

Think about the words you will use in your project. Will you handwrite your labels? Consider ways to use words that would add interest to your autobiography. You can use a computer to type explanations and narrative. You can use letters cut out from magazines. You can also use the resist process, by writing with oil pastels and painting over it with watercolor.

One of the wonders of painting is that we can always make changes, wipe out portions we don't like, or even start all over again. Our lives are much the same way. By revisiting the events of our lives with fresh eyes, we can reframe our stories to see the course of our lives in a more empowering way. We have the ability to discern and choose those interpretations that are life enhancing rather than destructive, and each time we shed an unnecessary or limiting belief we can renew ourselves. The Chinese Zen poet Shih-wu reminds us, "Events and hopes seldom agree, but who can step back doesn't worry."

Reflections

What did you learn from making your autobiography?

What did you see about your life that you hadn't seen before doing this project?

How will you live the rest of your life?

Conclusion

THE PAINTING PATH CONTINUES

We have walked this painting path together, from the first experimental drawings you did using oil pastels all the way through water-based oil paints. You have practiced pastel, watercolor, resist, batik, collage, and many other challenging and exciting projects. By this point, you have an idea which media call to you and which you would like to practice and pursue.

I chose to introduce the autobiography as our last project because you can use it as the culmination of all the painting techniques you have learned and explored in this book. You might even consider chapter 11 your "graduation project" whereby you can combine techniques and let your imagination go wild.

Oil painting seemed a fitting project for the penultimate chapter of this book because it has been the most popular medium throughout art history, and most paintings in museums are done in oils. In a way, it is the richest, most monumental means of expression of paint on a surface. I suggest that you do some more oil paintings. Buy some canvases of assorted sizes and try different projects.

Set up a still life, as you did in chapter 5 using pastels, and try to paint it in oils. Try a self-portrait in oil paints, using the same basic instructions in the self-portrait chapter. Sketch your face using washes of color that dry quickly. Build up the surface using thicker paint that you mix with linseed oil to help it blend well. Look at self-portraits in oil by van Gogh, Kahlo, Cézanne, Matisse, Degas, and Rembrandt. Get inspired by the great works of the masters!

Don't be surprised if you fall in love with pastel for a period of time and then switch to watercolor and fall in love with that for a while. However you do it, you are walking the path of the painter. This path has been trodden by many before us.

My wish for all of us is that we stay connected to that inner voice and let it guide us on our journey.

Resources

Throughout the writing of this book I've been inspired by many books about art, yoga, and spirituality. Below you will find resources to deepen your knowledge about yoga, art techniques, spiritual discovery, and inspirational artists. I've divided them into a few basic categories for easy reference. My hope is that these books will enhance your appreciation for the topics you've explored in *The Painting Path*.

PASTEL

Handell, Albert, and Anita West. *Painting the Landscape in Pastel.* New York: Watson-Guptill, 2000.

Handell, Albert, and Leslie Trainor. *Intuitive Light: An Emotional Approach to Capturing the Illusion of Value, Form, Color and Space.* New York: Watson-Guptill, 2003.

Mowry, Elizabeth. *Landscape Meditations: An Artist's Guide to Exploring Themes in Landscape Painting.* New York: Watson-Guptill, 2005.

———. *The Pastelist's Year: Painting the Four Seasons in Pastel.* New York: Watson-Guptill, 2001.

WATERCOLOR

Cooper, Helen A. *Winslow Homer Watercolors.* New Haven: Yale University Press, 1987.

Little, Carl. *The Watercolors of John Singer Sargent.* Berkeley: University of California Press, 1999.

Miller, Henry. *To Paint Is to Love Again.* Alhambra, CA: Cambria Books, 1960.

Unger, Miles. *The Watercolors of Winslow Homer.* New York: W. W. Norton, 2001.

COLLAGE

Brommer, Gerald. *Collage Techniques: A Guide for Artists and Illustrators.* New York: Watson-Guptill, 1994.

BATIK

Tucker, Sarah. *Batik.* Wiltshire, UK: The Crowood Press, 1999.

YOGA AND SPIRIT

Cope, Stephen. *The Wisdom of Yoga: A Seeker's Guide to Extraordinary Living.* New York: Bantam Books, 2007.

———. *Yoga and the Quest for the True Self.* New York: Bantam Books, 2000.

Faulds, Richard. *Kripalu Yoga: A Guide to Practice On and Off the Mat.* New York: Bantam Books, 2006.

———. *Sayings of Swami Kripalu: Inspiring Quotes from a Contemporary Yoga Master.* Kearney, NE: Morris Publishing, 2004.

Krishnamurti, Jiddu. *Freedom from the Known.* San Francisco: HarperSanFrancisco, 1975.

Levitt, Atma Jo Ann. *Pilgrim Of Love: The Life And Teachings Of Swami Kripalu.* Rhinebeck, NY: Monkfish Book Publishing, 2004.

Suzuki, Shunryu. *Zen Mind, Beginner's Mind.* New York: Walker/Weatherhill, 1970.

POETRY

Barks, Coleman, trans. *The Essential Rumi.* San Francisco: HarperSanFrancisco, 1995.

Faulds, Danna. *Go In and In: Poems from the Heart of Yoga.* Kearney, NE: Morris Publishing, 2002.

———. *Prayers to the Infinite: New Yoga Poems.* Kearney, NE: Morris Publishing, 2004.

DVDS

Cope, Stephen. *Kripalu Yoga Dynamic.* DVD, 84 minutes. Directed by William Swotes. Stockbridge, MA: Kripalu Yoga, 2005.

Lundeen, Sudha Carolyn. *Kripalu Yoga Gentle.* DVD, 85 minutes. Directed by William Swotes. Stockbridge, MA: Kripalu Yoga, 2005.

WEBSITES

ART

www.artchive.com

A lively survey of art history offering a timeline and a wealth of information about art through the ages, including hundreds of images. See especially the entry on Edward Hopper, the nineteenth-century oil painter and watercolorist mentioned in the Introduction.

www.artistsmagazine.com

A wonderful resource that offers workshops, art materials, and excellent instruction for artists with all levels of experience.

www.artlex.com

A comprehensive dictionary including everything you need to know about art: artists, media, art vocabulary, quotations, and more.

www.artschools.com

An excellent guide to art school throughout the United States, including museum schools and colleges offering instruction in all kinds of fine arts programs.

www.jssgallery.org

An extraordinary site devoted to the artist John Singer Sargent, an eighteenth-century American watercolorist and oil painter. Contains biographical information and a vast variety of images of his paintings (a feast for the eyes).

www.oilpastelsociety.com

A lively site devoted to the promotion of the knowledge and understanding of oil pastel as a fine art medium. Members can exhibit their own work in the society's shows.

www.painterskeys.com

A community for a wide community of creative people, including painters, sculptors, and writers, that also produces a twice-weekly newsletter. The website also contains a vast gallery of quotations by famous artists.

www.research.umbc.edu/~ivy/selfportrait/study.html

Wonderful pictures of famous self-portraits by many artists. Use this as inspiration for your own self-portraits.

www.vangoghgallery.com

The definitive online reference for information about the life and work of Vincent van Gogh. Presents biographical information, paintings, drawings, and quotations from this master.

YOGA AND SPIRIT

www.accesstoinsight.org/lib/authors/thanissaro/breathmed.html

Information about Buddhist meditation on the breath *(anapanasati)* that was discussed in chapter 5.

www.cuke.com

An archival site on the life and world of Shunryu Suzuki and those who knew him. This site also sells books by the great Zen monk.

www.jkrishnamurti.org

A wonderful site that abounds with biographical and philosophical information on the teachings of Krishnamurti, including an archive of "Talks and Dialogues" about his teachings.

www.kripalu.org

This website offers programs in yoga, meditation, and the arts presented at Kripalu Center in the Berkshire Mountains of Massachusetts. You can also use it to find yoga instructors in your area of the country.

www.rumi.net/rumi_by_shiva.htm

Be inspired by the life and poetry of the mystical poet, Rumi. An excellent resource for understanding his work.

Spirituality of the Seasons

Autumn: A Spiritual Biography of the Season
Edited by Gary Schmidt and Susan M. Felch; Illustrations by Mary Azarian
Rejoice in autumn as a time of preparation and reflection. Includes Wendell Berry, David James Duncan, Robert Frost, A. Bartlett Giamatti, E. B. White, P. D. James, Julian of Norwich, Garret Keizer, Tracy Kidder, Anne Lamott, May Sarton.
6 x 9, 320 pp, 5 b/w illus., Quality PB, 978-1-59473-118-1 **$18.99**
HC, 978-1-59473-005-4 **$22.99**

Spring: A Spiritual Biography of the Season
Edited by Gary Schmidt and Susan M. Felch; Illustrations by Mary Azarian
Explore the gentle unfurling of spring and reflect on how nature celebrates rebirth and renewal. Includes Jane Kenyon, Lucy Larcom, Harry Thurston, Nathaniel Hawthorne, Noel Perrin, Annie Dillard, Martha Ballard, Barbara Kingsolver, Dorothy Wordsworth, Donald Hall, David Brill, Lionel Basney, Isak Dinesen, Paul Laurence Dunbar. 6 x 9, 352 pp, 6 b/w illus., HC, 978-1-59473-114-3 **$21.99**

Summer: A Spiritual Biography of the Season
Edited by Gary Schmidt and Susan M. Felch; Illustrations by Barry Moser
"A sumptuous banquet.... These selections lift up an exquisite wholeness found within an everyday sophistication."— ★ *Publishers Weekly* starred review
Includes Anne Lamott, Luci Shaw, Ray Bradbury, Richard Selzer, Thomas Lynch, Walt Whitman, Carl Sandburg, Sherman Alexie, Madeleine L'Engle, Jamaica Kincaid.
6 x 9, 304 pp, 5 b/w illus., Quality PB, 978-1-59473-183-9 **$18.99**
HC, 978-1-59473-083-2 **$21.99**

Winter: A Spiritual Biography of the Season
Edited by Gary Schmidt and Susan M. Felch; Illustrations by Barry Moser
"This outstanding anthology features top-flight nature and spirituality writers on the fierce, inexorable season of winter.... Remarkably lively and warm, despite the icy subject." — ★ *Publishers Weekly* starred review.
Includes Will Campbell, Rachel Carson, Annie Dillard, Donald Hall, Ron Hansen, Jane Kenyon, Jamaica Kincaid, Barry Lopez, Kathleen Norris, John Updike, E. B. White.
6 x 9, 288 pp, 6 b/w illus., Deluxe PB w/flaps, 978-1-893361-92-8 **$18.95**
HC, 978-1-893361-53-9 **$21.95**

Spirituality / Animal Companions

Blessing the Animals: Prayers and Ceremonies to Celebrate God's Creatures, Wild and Tame   *Edited by Lynn L. Caruso* 5 x 7¼, 256 pp, HC, 978-1-59473-145-7 **$19.99**
What Animals Can Teach Us about Spirituality: Inspiring Lessons from Wild and Tame Creatures   *by Diana L. Guerrero* 6 x 9, 176 pp, Quality PB, 978-1-893361-84-3 **$16.95**

Spirituality & Crafts

The Knitting Way: A Guide to Spiritual Self-Discovery
by Linda Skolnik and Janice MacDaniels
7 x 9, 240 pp, Quality PB, b/w photographs, 978-1-59473-079-5 **$16.99**

The Quilting Path: A Guide to Spiritual Discovery through Fabric, Thread and Kabbalah
by Louise Silk
7 x 9, 192 pp, Quality PB, b/w photographs and illustrations, 978-1-59473-206-5 **$16.99**

The Scrapbooking Journey: A Hands-On Guide to Spiritual Discovery
by Cory Richardson-Lauve; Foreword by Stacy Julian
7 x 9, 176 pp, Quality PB, 8-page full-color insert, plus b/w photographs
978-1-59473-216-4 **$18.99**

Spiritual Practice

Divining the Body: Reclaim the Holiness of Your Physical Self
by Jan Phillips
A practical and inspiring guidebook for connecting the body and soul in spiritual practice. Leads you into a milieu of reverence, mystery and delight, helping you discover your body as a pathway to the Divine.
8 x 8, 256 pp, Quality PB, 978-1-59473-080-1 **$16.99**

Finding Time for the Timeless: Spirituality in the Workweek
by John McQuiston II
Simple, refreshing stories that provide you with examples of how you can refocus and enrich your daily life using prayer or meditation, ritual and other forms of spiritual practice. 5½ x 6¾, 208 pp, HC, 978-1-59473-035-1 **$17.99**

The Gospel of Thomas: A Guidebook for Spiritual Practice
by Ron Miller; Translations by Stevan Davies
An innovative guide to bring a new spiritual classic into daily life.
6 x 9, 160 pp, Quality PB, 978-1-59473-047-4 **$14.99**

Earth, Water, Fire, and Air: Essential Ways of Connecting to Spirit
by Cait Johnson 6 x 9, 224 pp, HC, 978-1-893361-65-2 **$19.95**

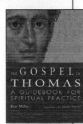

Labyrinths from the Outside In: Walking to Spiritual Insight—A Beginner's Guide
by Donna Schaper and Carole Ann Camp
6 x 9, 208 pp, b/w illus. and photos, Quality PB, 978-1-893361-18-8 **$16.95**

Practicing the Sacred Art of Listening: A Guide to Enrich Your Relationships
and Kindle Your Spiritual Life—The Listening Center Workshop
by Kay Lindahl 8 x 8, 176 pp, Quality PB, 978-1-893361-85-0 **$16.95**

Releasing the Creative Spirit: Unleash the Creativity in Your Life
by Dan Wakefield 7 x 10, 256 pp, Quality PB, 978-1-893361-36-2 **$16.95**

The Sacred Art of Bowing: Preparing to Practice
by Andi Young 5½ x 8½, 128 pp, b/w illus., Quality PB, 978-1-893361-82-9 **$14.95**

The Sacred Art of Chant: Preparing to Practice
by Ana Hernández 5½ x 8½, 192 pp, Quality PB, 978-1-59473-036-8 **$15.99**

The Sacred Art of Fasting: Preparing to Practice
by Thomas Ryan, CSP 5½ x 8½, 192 pp, Quality PB, 978-1-59473-078-8 **$15.99**

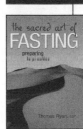

The Sacred Art of Forgiveness: Forgiving Ourselves and Others through God's Grace
by Marcia Ford 8 x 8, 176 pp, Quality PB, 978-1-59473-175-4 **$16.99**

The Sacred Art of Listening: Forty Reflections for Cultivating a Spiritual Practice
by Kay Lindahl; Illustrations by Amy Schnapper
8 x 8, 160 pp, b/w illus., Quality PB, 978-1-893361-44-7 **$16.99**

The Sacred Art of Lovingkindness: Preparing to Practice
by Rabbi Rami Shapiro; Foreword by Marcia Ford
5½ x 8½, 176 pp, Quality PB, 978-1-59473-151-8 **$16.99**

Sacred Speech: A Practical Guide for Keeping Spirit in Your Speech
by Rev. Donna Schaper 6 x 9, 176 pp, Quality PB, 978-1-59473-068-9 **$15.99**
HC, 978-1-893361-74-4 **$21.95**

About SKYLIGHT PATHS Publishing

SkyLight Paths Publishing is creating a place where people of different spiritual traditions come together for challenge and inspiration, a place where we can help each other understand the mystery that lies at the heart of our existence.

Through spirituality, our religious beliefs are increasingly becoming a part of our lives—rather than *apart* from our lives. While many of us may be more interested than ever in spiritual growth, we may be less firmly planted in traditional religion. Yet, we do want to deepen our relationship to the sacred, to learn from our own as well as from other faith traditions, and to practice in new ways.

SkyLight Paths sees both believers and seekers as a community that increasingly transcends traditional boundaries of religion and denomination—people wanting to learn from each other, *walking together, finding the way.*

For your information and convenience, at the back of this book we have provided a list of other SkyLight Paths books you might find interesting and useful. They cover the following subjects:

Buddhism / Zen	Gnosticism	Mysticism
Catholicism	Hinduism /	Poetry
Children's Books	Vedanta	Prayer
Christianity	Inspiration	Religious Etiquette
Comparative	Islam / Sufism	Retirement
Religion	Judaism / Kabbalah /	Spiritual Biography
Current Events	Enneagram	Spiritual Direction
Earth-Based	Meditation	Spirituality
Spirituality	Midrash Fiction	Women's Interest
Global Spiritual	Monasticism	Worship
Perspectives		

Or phone, fax, mail or e-mail to: SKYLIGHT PATHS Publishing
Sunset Farm Offices, Route 4 • P.O. Box 237 • Woodstock, Vermont 05091
Tel: (802) 457-4000 • Fax: (802) 457-4004 • www.skylightpaths.com
Credit card orders: (800) 962-4544 (8:30AM–5:30PM ET Monday–Friday)
Generous discounts on quantity orders. SATISFACTION GUARANTEED. Prices subject to change.

For more information about each book,
visit our website at www.skylightpaths.com